Praise for *In on it: What adoptive parents wou* _____
about adoption

Praise from relatives and friends of adoptive families:

Written with humor and honesty, we found *In on it* to be very helpful and instructive. We are in agreement: we feel more protective toward our coming grandchild and more involved in the adoption after reading *In on it*.

—Gary and Chris, grandparents-to-be, Kansas

In on it helped me to better understand the adoption experience of a dear friend of mine and what her adoptive parents experienced. It provides helpful suggestions and ideas of ways I can be more involved and supportive of adoptive parents and their children.

—Kelly B., close friend to several adoptive families, Iowa

In on it sparked surprising and meaningful conversations about adoption issues. It touched on subjects that were important to a shared understanding of adoption and the heartfelt discussions that resulted strengthened our connection as mother and daughter. We recommend *In on it* to any friends or relatives who want to understand adoption and support adoptive families in their incredible journey.

—Del and Judith, grandmother- and mother-to-be,
Florida and Minnesota

I enjoyed *In on it* more than I can say. I found it enlightening and welcoming. As a future adoptive grandmother, it's an adoption book written with me in mind.

—Kathi, grandmother-to-be, Washington

In on it is a much-needed and appreciated tool for adoptive parents, relatives and friends. It is insightful, educational and thought-provoking. I strongly recommend it to anyone considering adopting and to their family and friends.
> —Carolyn, grandmother, Florida

As an adoptive mother, I found *In on it* to be a wonderful tool for introducing friends and relatives to our adoption.

As a grandmother, though adoption is not unfamiliar to me, *In on it* offered new insights and understanding, as well as an opening for conversations around sensitive adoption topics.

We both strongly recommend *In on it* to other families and their loved ones lucky enough to be touched by adoption.
> —Tania and Joan, new mother and grandmother,
> California

Praise from adoptive parents for *In on it:*

In on it made me realize that, in my haste to adopt, I had overlooked the needs of my extended family. They need time to think about and process the changes taking place. This is why *In on it* is so important. It made me both cry and smile. I see it becoming a must-read for all of those in the "adoption circle."
> —Lara, adoptive mother, Alabama

A fantastic read. I want to buy a box full of this guide and put it on our doorstep! It's a great guide for *everyone* in the adoption circle.
> —Rhonda, mother-to-be, California

In on it is a great resource for friends and family of those who have adopted or are in the process of adopting. I can't wait to share this book with my own friends and relatives.
> —Kelly G., mother-to-be, Iowa

In on it is very informative, easy to read, and filled with helpful suggestions and insights. An excellent resource for the friends and family of anyone who has adopted or is adopting.

—Dana, expectant adoptive mother, Kansas

I wish I could have everyone I know read this book! It's a great introduction to adoption, especially for people who want to know how to help and support an adoptive family.

—Tamra, expectant adoptive mother, Ohio

A wonderful read, sensitively written, full of important information. We wish we'd had it to give our son's grandparents when we adopted.

—Krista and Philip, parents, New York

Praise from adoption professionals for *In on it*:

Elisabeth O'Toole's clear, insightful, and comprehensive guide to adoption is written expressly for and *to* a readership generally overlooked: the extended family and friends of new adoptive parents. Grandparents and neighbors anxious about what to say or do will be heartened by this fine book's conversational tone and generous spirit. They'd be wise to accept the welcome into "the adoption circle" that *In on it* extends. And adoptive families will be glad they cared enough to read it.

—Cheri Register, author of *"Are Those Kids Yours?" American Families with Children Adopted from Other Countries* and *Beyond Good Intentions: A Mother Reflects on Raising Internationally Adopted Children."*

Excellent. Practical and sensitive wisdom for anyone supporting a loved one's adoption process.

—Corrie L. Wold, MSW, LISW, Information and Education Director, Children's Home Society and Family Services, Minneapolis

Elisabeth O'Toole addresses the complex and emotional experience of adoption with humor and respect, opening a path for friends and relatives to become insiders to the process. *In on it* is a well-written resource for people who want to support their loved ones, but aren't always sure what to do or say. This book will remain on my "recommended reading" list for adoptive families and their friends.

—Janna Annest, adoptive parent and adoption law columnist, *Adoptive Families Magazine*

A needed reference for families and friends.

—Abbie Smith, LCSW, Director of Clinical Services, Holt International, Eugene (OR)

In on it demonstrates how adoption is something both ordinary and extraordinary. The author, an adoptive parent herself, speaks to her readers with optimism, sensitivity and humor.

—Emily Hollidge, LICSW, family therapist

In on it:

What adoptive parents would like you to know about adoption

A Guide for Relatives and Friends

ELISABETH O'TOOLE

Fig Press • St. Paul, Minnesota

Published by:
Fig Press
St. Paul, Minnesota
www.InOnAdoption.com

WHO'S MY PRETTY BABY
Words and Music by Woody Guthrie
TRO-© Copyright 1964 (Renewed) Ludlow Music, Inc., New York, NY
International Copyright Secured
Made in U.S.A
All Rights Reserved Including Public Performance For Profit
Used by permission
Lyrics cited are not entirely the original lyrics of the song.

Omaha Indian prayer is used with the permission of the Smithsonian
Institution.

Cover design by Amy Kirkpatrick, Kirkpatrick Design
Interior design by Dorie McClelland, Spring Book Design

ISBN: 978-0-9828765-0-3

Printed in the United States of America

This is for you three.

Who'll be my little man
Who'll be my nice lady
Who'll be my funny little bunny, hey hey, pretty babe.

You'll be my little man
You'll be my nice lady
You'll be my funny little bunny, hey hey, pretty babe.

—Woody Guthrie, "Who's my pretty baby"

Contents

Sun, moon, stars,
you that move in the heavens,
hear this mother!
A new child has come among you.
Make its life smooth.

—Omaha Indian ceremony for children
Smithsonian Institution Press

Introduction

People in grocery stores

O ne afternoon, while I was wandering through the neighborhood grocery store with my son, an elderly woman approached us. White-haired and cardigan-sweat-ered, she was the whole package: Sweet Little Old Lady. She looked intently at my baby, who was calmly surveying things from the seat of our grocery cart, then at me, happily bask-ing in my new motherhood, and said, "Look at that beauti-ful skin. Is he adopted?"

Sigh. I was just there to pick up some fruit. Maybe a loaf of bread. I opened my mouth to respond with an irritable "You know, that is really none of your business." And stopped. Having spent my formative years being told repeat-edly to mind my manners, I had developed a Pavlovian response to respecting my elders, even the annoying ones. In my family, you didn't get to tell anyone older than your old-est sibling what you really thought of them.

So, as it usually does, good manners won out. She was old. I wanted bananas. Today was not going to be the day

I played adoption educator. I braced myself for some silly follow-up question about adoption ("What is he?" or "Does he speak Spanish?") and answered, "As a matter of fact, he *was*." Then I fixed her with my best "What of it?" stare.

"Oh!" She said happily, and grabbed one of my crossed arms. "My niece is adopting a daughter from China. We are all so excited for her. She's on pins and needles. It's just so hard for us to wait!" I relaxed. (And felt a little sheepish.) That's all she had wanted to say: that she was in on it, too. Five minutes later she had shown me how to pick a ripe cantaloupe and knew my son by name. Thank goodness for good manners.

As a new mother, this incident was instructive. I realized that though people will wonder (sometimes aloud) about my family, they almost always mean well. The lady in the grocery store might have taken a different approach (perhaps simply mentioning her niece's adoption, allowing me the option to decide whether or not to mention my own); but she was obviously well-intentioned and, most important, clearly happy for and supportive of her niece and the coming child.

As a friend or relative of an adoptive family, you're in on something now. You, too, might be so excited at the prospect of welcoming the child into your life that you want to share your enthusiasm with fellow shoppers and their babies. Or perhaps you've found you have reservations about adoption; maybe you're even feeling some disappointment around it.

You might be wondering how you can best help your loved ones or whether there's even a role for you in your loved one's adoption. You might be having all of these feelings—among others—at the same time. Know that you're not the only one who has felt this way about the adoption. In fact, the adoptive parents were once newly in on it, too. They, too, might have been both excited and scared, eager and reluctant. Adoption is like that.

When my husband and I first began sharing our plans to adopt, I remember being surprised by how often I was asked to explain both our decision to adopt and adoption in general. I was asked several times why we weren't adopting within the United States, when there were "so many babies who need families *right here*." People unfamiliar with adoption advised us that our adoptive children would likely be unhealthy, because their birthmothers would be on drugs, alcoholic or HIV positive. These reactions from strangers and acquaintances were unexpected—I hadn't anticipated needing to respond to public comment on what to me were fairly private, even intimate, matters.

But more important was the realization that, as part of our adoption preparation, we needed to be able to explain adoption and our choices around it to our families and friends: people who cared deeply about us and our prospective family. I learned that I couldn't just bristle if someone made an unfortunate comment or asked an inappropriate question. I began to understand that adoptive parents can't expect others—including those closest to them—to have had the opportunity to think through and become educated about all of the adoption-related issues that they themselves had to consider along the way to becoming parents. In fact, before they began their own adoption education, it's likely your loved ones made questionable comments and asked awkward questions about adoption, as well. I sure did.

Adoption was once very unfamiliar territory for my husband and me. When we first considered adoption, we'd had no adoptions in our immediate families and none of our close friends at the time had adopted. So my own adoption learning curve was steep. And when faced with something that both thrilled and scared me—as adoption once did—my response was to learn all I could about it. I read adoption book after adoption book. I attended every adoption seminar available and visited every adoption web site I could find. I talked to adoptive parents, people who had made an adoption plan for a child (*birthparents*), and individuals who were themselves adopted (*adoptees*). I gathered information and opinions. And the more informed and comfortable I became with adoption, the more my fears began to recede and my anticipation began to build.

Adoption was such an important, life-altering decision for us, and I wanted to share the experience with the people close to us. In fact, I felt I had a responsibility to share with my friends and loved ones some of what I was learning about adoption. These were people who would interact closely with our new family and who appreciated the opportunity to prepare for the adoption themselves. I found myself offering them abbreviated versions of the articles and books I was reading and the classes I was attending—almost all of them intended for adoptive parents only. I'd make copies of a few pages from an adoption book, or send a link to an article, sharing information about how adoptions are currently being conducted and about what is now expected of adoptive families. And some of these trends were difficult for people unfamiliar with contemporary adoption to digest. Sometimes I felt I was explaining (or defending) our adoption plans to the raised eyebrows of benevolent skeptics—people who wanted only the best for us, but whose general understanding of adoption was not in alignment with what I was telling them about it.

What I needed was a single book of general adoption information and insights that I could offer to those who wanted to participate in our adoption experience and in our lives as an adoptive family. It would familiarize them with adoption in general, and also serve as a starting point for conversations about our own adoption. It would explain the challenges, anticipations, and joys of contemporary adoption. I wouldn't expect others to read the long, parent-oriented adoption books that I did, but instead a book that spoke to them directly, as people closely connected to an adopting family, and that sought to address *their* needs and concerns around adoption.

The result is this book on adoption, written especially for you, the grandparents and friends, aunts and uncles, colleagues and neighbors of adoptive parents. There are a number of ways in which I hope you will find it useful.

First, this book offers you a way to acquire some of the same knowledge and insights about adoption that your loved ones have gained via their own adoption process. Much as they might want to, your loved ones may lack the time or capacity to download all that they are learning and deciding during what is an intensely personal and complicated process. Instead, this book can serve to familiarize you independently with some of what your loved ones may consider and encounter, both en route to parenthood and as an adoptive family. I suspect most parents will be grateful to you for your genuine interest in their adoption, as demonstrated by your willingness to learn about it both from them and on your own.

Second—and your loved ones may not yet have had the chance to consider this themselves—the adoption will affect *you*. Some of these effects may be subtle and only recognizable over time. Others may be obvious and immediate. One very common way friends and relatives are affected by an adoption is that they may be called upon to speak on behalf of adoption and the adoptive family. You may be asked questions or receive comments—about the child, the family, and adoption in general—to which you'll want to be prepared to respond with care and insight. This book can help you do so.

Third, adoption will have an ongoing role in the life of the family. Ultimately, most families formed through adoption are like any other family: a mix of over-scheduled, occasionally combative individuals who adore one another. And you will likely find that's generally how you will come to think of them. But it's also true that there are particular issues and concerns—and delights—that accompany this route to parenthood. Adoption—like an adoptive family—is both ordinary and, well, extraordinary. Some familiarity with the ways that various aspects of adoption may be treated within the family can offer you both guidance and reassurance.

Finally, and perhaps most importantly, someone you care about is offering you the opportunity to participate in their lives, perhaps even including you in their adoption process. This book suggests ways to be informed and involved—from providing support to a waiting family, to assisting with the transitions of a new family, to appreciating the ongoing privilege of adoption in the lives of your loved ones over time.

It was once standard to consider adoption and adoption issues only in terms of an adoption *triad*: the birthmother, the child, and the adoptive parents. Now, the adoption community recognizes a broader *constellation* of people touched by adoption, often called the *adoption circle*—all of the friends and relatives, teachers and neighbors, congregants and colleagues that may witness and support an adoption—and who may themselves impact the adoptive family. That's you—a part of someone's adoption circle, a member of the constellation of adoption. And you have a lot to look forward to.

Before you begin

In writing this book, I gathered the advice and experiences of adoptive parents, birthparents, adoptees, adoption social workers and attorneys, and friends and relatives of adoptive families. They shared their contributions via discussion groups, questionnaires, personal interviews and their own writing on adoption. Their contributions revealed that, while every family's adoption is wonderfully unique (and that almost every adoptive parent smiles as they tell their family's adoption story), there are certain commonalities to the experience of adoption. There are standard challenges and opportunities to be expected, typical frustrations and joys, and universal advice pertinent to the adoption circle of almost any adoptive family. (Oddly, many adoptive parents have their own grocery store incident to recount; ask your loved ones.)

I hope this book can suggest for you some of what your friends or relatives have experienced or are experiencing on their adoption journey. Many of the anecdotes and insights discussed here will resonate with you and your loved ones; others may not. This is as it should be. Your experience with an adoption will be very much your own. My hope is that, besides providing useful information and insights, this book also prompts questions and conversations between you and your loved ones. Because their perspective on adoption is really the most important.

Note that this book is intended to *introduce* you—friends and relatives—to adoption. If there's a particular adoption issue that you would like to know about in more detail than is provided here (e.g., open adoption, older child adoption, transracial adoption, building attachment), there are many helpful books, web sites, and organizations devoted to specific topics in adoption. A list of resources at the end of the book offers some suggestions.

For the purposes of simplicity and clarity, the book generally refers to adoptive parents (plural) and the adoptive child (singular). Of course many adoptions entail a single parent or more than one child, and this book is meant to encompass their perspectives as well.

Finally, you're reading this book because you want to share in the experience of your loved ones who are adopting or have adopted. You may have questions about how best to do so. Throughout the book you'll find lists of specific suggestions and ideas for helping and supporting your loved ones. To that end, following are some ideas for things you can do right now to show your interest and begin to participate in their lives as an adoptive family.

What you can do

Offer to share the adoption journey with the adoptive parents. Let them know that you're reading this book or otherwise educating yourself about adoption.

Encourage them to see your perspective. Remind them that adoption was once new to them, too.

You may need to take some risks. Part of being involved

and supportive will include asking and talking about adoption. If you are unsure about how to discuss adoption, this book offers information and insights that can make you feel more confident when you do. But give yourself permission to inadvertently say what may be interpreted as the "wrong" thing. Everyone—including adoptive parents—does.

Understand that at times the adoptive parents may be sensitive about the subject of adoption and their child. At times adoption may be a touchy topic for the adoptive parents, especially if they're still becoming comfortable with it themselves.

Maybe you feel you've made mistakes in the past or said things you regret. Consider making an apology if you think one is warranted. Tell your loved ones you're trying to learn more about adoption. Forgive yourself and move on.

Be open to learning and growing.

1

Deciding to adopt

When my husband and I began to share our decision to adopt, we received a wide range of reactions. They ranged from "Congratulations!" (a lovely reaction) to "Are you sure you've tried *everything* to have a baby of your own?" (ouch) to "Oh, now you'll definitely get pregnant" (no, no, no).

How did you feel when you learned your loved ones were adopting? Maybe you were relieved that they were finally going to satisfy a long-held desire to become parents, or thrilled at the prospect of a new child joining the family. Maybe you felt fear or confusion about their plans to adopt. Maybe you were unaware that adoption was even a consideration for them. You may have been reluctant to accept their decision as final. One adoptive mother recounts how her mother, when informed of her adoption plans, asked whether her daughter had considered trying to get pregnant via her best (male, gay) friend instead. Other parents recall being asked "Why?" and "Are you sure?" when they shared their news. It's likely you felt—and may continue to feel—a complicated convergence of emotions: fear and anticipation, worry and relief, gratitude and disappointment. It's not unusual or unreasonable to feel some ambivalence. Understanding *why* and *how* your loved ones chose adoption may help to alleviate some of your reservations, should you have them.

Why they've decided to adopt

People decide to adopt for many reasons. Some parents have a desire to expand their family and, though they could have—and perhaps do have—biological children, they also want to parent children who already exist and need families. There may be religious, political, and philosophical drivers behind an adoption. Prospective parents may be drawn to removing an adoptable child from foster care and into a permanent family. People may be moved to adopt for humanitarian reasons, in response to dire economic and social conditions around the world, or in reaction to the needs of a country in crisis. Single people and same-sex couples often find adoption their most realistic path to parenthood. Sometimes foster parents find they want to adopt a foster child. Others come to adoption through a family circumstance and end up adopting a relative (*kinship adoption*).

A very common impetus for adoption is infertility. According to research by the Evan B. Donaldson Adoption Institute, more than 80% of people adopting through an adoption agency or independently (using an adoption attorney) cite infertility as their initial reason for adopting. About

50% of those adopting through foster care cite infertility as an impetus.

Several adoptive parents discussed with me their decision to contend with the challenge of infertility privately, sometimes declining to share it even with those very close to them. If this was the case with your loved ones, their decision to adopt may have come as a surprise to you. One adoptive parent recalled her mother's reaction to her adoption announcement, asking, "Have you seen a doctor?" She assured her mother that she had seen a doctor—that she had in fact seen *many* doctors. If your loved ones are adopting after infertility, the prospective parents have likely tried to investigate and address it, at least to the extent of protecting their basic health. Now they are ready to move forward in a different way. If someone has been private about their fertility issues, try not to take it personally. It's a common approach to what's often a vulnerable time for people.

Also, it should not be assumed that every parent will go to any length, try any procedure, to have a genetic connection to their child. It's important to some people and unimportant to others. One parent of both an adoptive son and a biological son remarked that others tend to assume that she adopted her first child because she'd been infertile. In actuality, she'd just wanted to begin her family through adoption. Similarly, and like many other adoptive parents, my husband and I once anticipated creating a family comprised of both biological and adoptive children. Once we realized that my sturdy build, general good health and an ethnic stereotype of rampant fertility were not going to be enough to ensure a biological child ("Seriously? With these hips?"), my husband and I began pursuing adoption only.

If infertility is a reason for adoption, understand that *adoption is not conceding defeat.* Rather, adoption is committing to another path. At this point, whether or not adoption was your loved ones' initial choice for achieving parenthood no longer really matters.

Even if you don't know the specific reasons behind an adoption, know that almost no one decides to adopt without having considered their options—adoption among them—for achieving parenthood. Besides adoption, the prospective parents may have considered resolving fertility problems (should they exist); foster-parenting; maintaining their current family size; even permanent childlessness. The adoptive parents may have even pursued some of these other options prior to deciding to adopt. Regardless of why your loved ones decided to adopt, know that thorough consideration and self-examination likely preceded their decision to do so.

Before committing to adoption

Your loved ones' adoption was not the product of a single decision—to adopt or not to adopt. Rather it was the result of many decisions and choices, some fairly simple, some no doubt extremely difficult. Making the decision to adopt is its own journey. It's a mental and emotional precedent to the physical process of adoption that follows. Here is just some of what your loved ones have likely considered before arriving at "We'll adopt."

Your loved ones have contemplated their own ability to parent a child who is genetically unrelated to them, potentially of another race, probably past infancy, and possibly with health, behavioral or developmental issues. They may have had to evaluate the impact an adoption might have on their other children. People who adopt as a single person have evaluated their own capacity to bear alone the responsibilities of parenthood. Both single adoptive parents and same-sex adoptive parents have had to consider their ability to provide role models and relationships with adults of another gender. Parents have considered their willingness to sustain a relationship with birthparents or birth relatives. All prospective adoptive parents should have carefully considered the practical, financial, social and emotional realities and responsibilities of parenting through adoption and their own abilities to meet them.

Your loved ones have learned that they will be required to meet and overcome many challenges to reach parenthood in this way. These challenges reside somewhere on the continuum between *mildly annoying* and *utterly demoralizing*. Detailed personal histories of each parent must be documented. Financial and medical records must be collected and presented. Any health or legal wrinkle in an adoptive parent's past must be recounted and defended (e.g., even things like driving violations from decades ago may need to be explained). Paperwork gets lost and has to be completed again. Strangers enter the home asking personal questions and counting smoke detectors. Birthparents may meet and decline prospective adoptive parents. Adoptions may be disrupted or fail before they are legally concluded. For international adoptions, additional country-specific requirements must be met. Some countries set age limits on the adoptive parents. Others require that parents meet specific health standards. Many countries—including certain states in the United States—limit or even prohibit adoptions by single or same-sex parents. Political and societal events occurring in other parts of the world or changes in relationships between governments can result in countries "closing" to outside adoptions, leaving waiting families—and children—in limbo. Adoptive parents quickly learn that any of this—or all of this—may await them when they decide to adopt.

So most adoptive parents have completed a painstaking decision-making process before committing to adoption, and they are evidently willing to accept the many potential challenges that can arise. They've decided they are willing to work hard—harder than they probably once expected—to achieve parenthood through adoption.

There is a wonderful consequence to all of this deliberation: the adoptive parents have likely become quite conscious of why and how much they want to parent the child they will adopt. Your loved ones can be better parents to their child for having a heightened awareness of their reasons for becoming so. As a friend or relative, this can reassure you. The opportunity to gain that kind of consciousness about parenthood is a gift.

**They've decided to adopt in a certain way:
the one that works for them**

Another adoption decision has to do with *how* the parents
want to adopt. Your loved ones have had to determine the
type of adoption they want to pursue and the type of child
they are willing to adopt. To get a sense of their experience,
imagine how you might respond to the following list of
questions:

*Could you parent a child of a different race? Which races
specifically? Could you parent a child from another country?
Which countries? Could you parent a child in contact with
the birthmother? Birthfather? Birth grandparents? Siblings?
Could you parent a child with physical disabilities? Which ones
exactly? How about mental disabilities? Could you parent more
than one child? An older child? How old? What about a child
who has been neglected or abused?*

Until I faced these decisions, I had never thought so
specifically about adoption—or parenthood, for that matter.
If anything, I had a vague, untested belief that I could parent
any child who was in need of a family. And I really wanted to
be that person, someone who could handle any obstacle with
equanimity, one with boundless patience and humor, able to
provide with generous hands whatever my child needed from
me. I still want to be that person. But I'm not. It was only
by considering adoption myself—by facing that checklist
in front of me on the dining room table (I can still picture
it)—that I was compelled to acknowledge and accept my
own capacities and limitations as a potential parent. Forcing

myself to be very honest about what I *could* provide was not only for my own good, but also for the good of my future children. I couldn't adopt *any* child. In fact, no one should adopt *any* child. Every family needs to adopt in the way that's best for them and their family, and thereby best for the adoptive child. So it's important that you, who want to support the family, know that most parents have done the work to decide what they can provide for a child, and, accordingly, determined the type of adoption to pursue.

Other decisions they've made

One of the early, primary decisions all prospective adoptive parents need to make is whether and how they would manage the additional responsibilities of adopting a child of another race or ethnicity—transracial adoption. This type of adoption is becoming more and more common, particularly as children of color comprise an ever-growing segment of the population of adoptable children, both domestically and around the world. In fact, a 2007 study by the U.S. Department of Health and Human Services found that almost half of children adopted domestically or internationally are of a race or culture other than that of their parents.

I once believed that race didn't matter when adopting and parenting—all that mattered was that children and parents love each other. My adoption training and early experience as a mother has taught me that this approach was very simplistic. Indeed, my husband and I had to decide that we were willing to try to meet additional responsibilities when we decided to adopt transracially. Part of our job as our children's parents is to try to provide models and experiences for them that reflect and support not only our family but also their own origins and the diversity of the world in which they live. Your loved ones will have made decisions regarding transracial adoption, too. (Transracial adoption is discussed further in *chapter 4—Digging deeper: Beyond the paperwork*.)

Another aspect of adoption that prospective adoptive parents must consider is their willingness to participate in an *open* adoption. These are adoptions in which there are varying levels of contact between birthparent and adoptive family. An open adoption can be a very uncomfortable concept if, as was mine, your understanding of adoption was based on an expectation of total separation of the child and birthmother or even secrecy around an adoption. Indeed, this was once the norm.

I vividly recall sitting in an early adoption meeting and learning from a social worker that we would be strongly encouraged to have some contact with our future child's birthmother. My immediate reaction was resistance and fear. I remember thinking there was no way I would ever participate in an open adoption. I mean, come on. Wouldn't it confuse the child? And be a threat to me and my family? Was I never going to get to be a *real* mom?

That social worker had my full (defensive) attention. Good thing, because I learned that I, like many people, had some real misconceptions about open adoption. I learned that openness takes many forms and typically evolves over time. Some open adoptions limit contact between the family and birthmother to an annual exchange of pictures and letters. Others exchange presents at holidays and see each other regularly. After talking with families about open adoption and seeing this type of adoption in practice, I began to understand the continuum of openness and what it really meant, and I grew to understand how it could work and ultimately benefit an adoptive family. In fact, some adoptive parents want contact with a birthparent and are sorry they don't have it. Your loved ones, too, will have made initial decisions as to their stance on openness. (Open adoption is discussed further in *chapter 4—Digging deeper: Beyond the paperwork.*)

Prospective adoptive parents will make many decisions about the right type of adoption for their family. And they will sometimes have those decisions challenged. If they choose an open domestic adoption (adoptions that occur within a single country), others might question whether they wouldn't prefer the limited birthparent contact typically associated with an international adoption. Conversely, some observers (including some fellow adoptive parents) criticize the choice to pursue an international adoption when there are children available for adoption domestically. Others find it hard to understand why a family would adopt an older child instead of an infant. Or wait for an infant instead of choosing an available older child. One thing is clear: your loved ones will likely have formed at least initial answers to these questions for themselves. And they will appreciate it if others, especially those who will comprise their family's adoption circle, try to accept without judgment these highly personal decisions.

How to say this gently? It's about them. (Just them.)
One adoptive mother tells the story of her mother-in-law's reaction to the news of her and her husband's decision to adopt. This couple was not particularly invested in having a genetic relationship to their children. When they could not easily get pregnant, they decided against using any medical assistance to do so, instead quickly opting to adopt. The mother-in-law, on the other hand, was of the opinion that no scientific stone should be left unturned, no fertility drug left uninjected, in the pursuit of a biological child. When her son announced to her their decision to adopt, his mother asked repeatedly what efforts to get pregnant had or had not been made and why or why not. When the prospective father suggested that decisions about using medical interventions were a private health matter and not really any of his mother's business, she declared, "Of course it's my business. I am the grandmother! Why aren't you trying *harder*?"

This is a pretty extreme example of someone failing to separate her own preferences from those of her adult child. And, in her defense, it seems the prospective grandmother had become very emotionally involved in becoming one, probably imagining for herself a more conventional route to grandparenthood, resulting in the placement of a very particular kind of baby in her arms. It seems she really *really* wanted to be a grandparent; perhaps to the point of losing sight of her more immediate responsibilities to her son and daughter-in-law. Yet it makes sense that even the best-intentioned friends and relatives can let their own feelings and anxieties color how they respond to the approaching adoption.

Like the adoptive parents, you, too, may need to go through a process to fully accept and recognize the adoption for the (sometimes unexpected) privilege that it is. People need to move at their own pace when accepting something new and perhaps unexpected, as an adoption may be. In fact, when a couple considers adoption, each partner needs his or her own time to make the decision, often resulting in one wishing to move forward before the other is quite ready. But while you can't negate your own reservations and concerns, you'll probably be glad later if what the adopting family sees (and remembers) most prominently is your love and support.

Whatever the chosen path to parenthood—whether it's fertility treatments, open adoption, international adoption, transracial adoption, domestic adoption, infant adoption, sibling adoption, special needs adoption, or foster care— trust that your loved ones have considered many of the options available to them and made the right decisions for their family.

The important role friends and relatives play in the decision to adopt

You should know that as part of the decision-making process, prospective adoptive parents also think a lot about their friends and relatives. Your loved ones have looked at the families and communities into which they propose to bring an adoptive child and they've tried to anticipate some of the child's potential experiences within them. Single parents, who will bear the enormous responsibility of parenthood alone, have considered whether they will receive emotional support as well as physical help with needs like emergency childcare. They've also had to designate a guardian for the child should something happen to the parent. Most adoptive parents evaluate the capacity of those close to them to be part of the family's support network.

One adoptive father described the issues he and his partner considered when discussing how adoption would affect their extended families. Their concern was that his family—which had been very supportive of him and his partner in the past—might find it difficult to handle the heightened visibility of the same-sex relationship that would accompany their becoming parents. The couple discussed their concerns with the future grandparents, who acknowledged the potential for increased scrutiny, but supported their son's desire to expand his family nonetheless. Any adoptive parent might feel some anxiety around how their family will be received and accepted by others.

It's an important step for those contemplating adoption to consider the potential responses of their friends and relatives to their adoption. In fact, questions about the reactions of family and friends to the parents' adoption plans are standard in social worker interviews with prospective parents. Know that your own response to the adoption has likely been considered as your loved ones made their adoption decision.

After the decisions comes . . . the announcement

After all of this deliberation and decision-making, your loved ones were ready to begin sharing their plans. Going public with their decision to adopt is a big step for prospective parents. In conversations with adoptive parents, I was struck by how clearly many remember others' reactions to the news of their adoption. Even those who had adopted their children many years ago could still vividly recall what a particular parent or sister-in-law or friend said to them— both the good ("Finally, we'll get some diversity in this family!") and the not-so-good ("Are you sure you want to do that?").

Your loved ones likely thought carefully about how and when they would inform others of their adoption plans. Parents describe how they fretted over the response of a particular important person, often a parent (sometimes fearing their disappointment, like that of the aforementioned grandmother). Adoptive parents may be concerned about generational attitudes around issues of race or of stereotypes about children who were adopted. They often worry about how those issues may play into other people's reactions to their adoption plans. And people make their announcement at different stages of the adoption process. Some share the news at their first inkling that an adoption may be in their future. Others wait until an actual child or birthparent has been identified and matched with them.

Because much of the decision-making process around the adoption may have happened privately, as a friend or relative you may have felt unprepared to learn that your loved one was planning to adopt. The announcement itself may have come as a surprise to you.

Though it might be ideal that everyone responds to someone's news that "We're adopting!" with immediate enthusiasm, it's just not realistic, especially if it was truly unexpected news. If you didn't respond with celebration, it doesn't make you a bad person or bad grandparent or a bad friend. It may make sense to want more information before supporting a new approach. And it's natural to respond to such a momentous announcement by asking questions. So, as a friend or relative, a cautious or reluctant response to adoption is not unusual, especially because it involves those who are dear to you. Many people's concerns about adoption stem directly from their feelings of love and protectiveness for the adoptive parents.

You may need time and information and experience to become comfortable with—and excited about—the idea of adoption. That said, consider that once they've made a decision to adopt, adopting parents often find they already feel a parent's sense of protectiveness and loyalty to the child that awaits them, even one yet unknown to them. The child will begin to supersede others among the parents' priorities. One adoptive parent remembers her mother's reluctant response to news of her adoption plans ("But I really want you to experience having your own child") as a wonderful thing, because her reaction reassured her of her decision to adopt. In response to her mother's words, she felt immediately protective of the unmet child, and she remembers this moment as the first time she experienced a maternal response to the child.

When my husband and I announced to others our readiness to adopt, it was hard to have our decision met with an immediate challenge, as it occasionally was. What we wanted was to be reassured. When we sat on my aunt's couch and shared with her our intent to adopt, she went into another room and brought back a baby blanket, one that she had knit and then lain aside long ago until it could be matched with news of an awaited child. She recalls that I started to cry when she presented it to us and she worried that she'd somehow done the wrong thing. But I cried because she had, in this gentle way, affirmed the decision that had emerged from a challenging process. She'd believed in us. That blanket had been long-intended for our child, regardless of how he joined the family. This reassured me.

As a friend or family member, your support following the adoption announcement can be invaluable to the adoptive family. Try to affirm their decision. They've made a thoughtful choice, but it's still one with challenging consequences and an uncertain outcome. They may be a little scared. Your reassurance can help.

Even if you're not yet a full proponent of an adoption, there are gestures you can make that show support for your loved ones. Consider attending an adoption information meeting (many agencies hold these regularly). My parents joined me for a presentation by a family in an open adoption, and though they didn't walk away fully convinced of the value of open adoption, the shared experience gave us some common ground for discussing this sometimes challenging aspect of adoption. You might make a donation to an adoption agency or child welfare organization. These are tangible ways to show you care about the prospective parents, regardless of your current feelings about the adoption.

They know the risks. They've heard the stories.

I was surprised to discover that one response people have upon learning that someone is adopting is to tell the prospective parent what I've come to call an *Adoption Horror Story*. I recall a colleague's reaction to my news that I was adopting. He immediately began telling me about his nephew, adopted as a toddler and, according to my colleague, so angry and violent that his parents struggled to keep his younger siblings safe from him. Someone else recounted a detailed history of her neighbor's daughter, attributing the girl's drug use, unplanned pregnancy, and contentious relationship with her mother to the fact of her adoption. You get the idea: horror stories.

I suspect that these kinds of stories were somehow intended as well-meant warnings. And the people who repeat these stories may have genuine concern for the adoptive parents. Or they may have had an inaccurate understanding of adoption based on specific, sensational situations that are often highlighted in the media.

But be assured, these stories are unnecessary. Because in conjunction with their feelings of anticipation and excitement, most expectant adoptive parents are also a little afraid. As a part of the adoption process, your loved ones are warned again and again, both of serious potential setbacks in the adoption itself and of lifelong issues that adoption may bring to them and their children. Until that child is in their arms and the adoption itself legally and irrevocably finalized, waiting parents maintain some apprehension about their decision and the uncertainty of the future. Even after the family has been established, that fear and anxiety—though greatly diminished—may never totally go away. There's no need for others to suggest new issues for them to worry about. They're full up.

Knowing that your loved ones may be hearing plenty of *Adoption Horror Stories*, try to tell an *Adoption Success Story* instead. They're everywhere. One of the nicest things anyone ever said to me about adoption came from someone who was neither a friend nor family member. She was someone I knew only in passing but who had learned that I was an adoptive mother. She told me, "I was adopted. And it was wonderful. Adoption is a big part of my life. I've thought about my birth family, and I've had questions and grief about my adoption. But my parents are amazing. I love them very much." Talk about reassuring. This compassionate person anticipated some of my worries and took it upon herself as an insider to reassure me. Because adoption *is* scary at first, and adoptive parents *are* worried. They can always use more reassurance. So leave the *Horror Stories* to people who don't know any better, and instead, bring on the *Success Stories*.

Congratulations: an opportunity awaits you

If your initial reaction to the adoption news was not what you or the adoptive parents might have liked, acknowledge it, consider apologizing or explaining to the parents, let them know you're interested in learning more, and move on. Even if you still have reservations or concerns—and they may be legitimate—your congratulations are appropriate and will be appreciated and remembered.

Then offer a listening ear. I remember working through a lot of adoption worries with my father during regular walks with our dogs. I don't remember anything we discussed in particular. But I remember he would ask me sensible (and sometimes difficult) questions and then give me space to refine my answers. I remember looking forward to those walks, knowing I had a safe place to process information and decisions without judgment.

In fact, a lovely byproduct of an adoption may be the deepening and strengthening of relationships with the people who help and support their loved ones as they are en route to becoming parents. Friendly relationships can turn into real friendships. Family bonds can deepen and mature as adult children—the adopting parents—share their adoption experience with parents and siblings. As a friend or relative of an adoptive family, you have the chance to be a part of something that will change everything for your loved ones. An adoption is a time of great opportunity for your relationship with them.

What you can do

Attend a general adoption information session at a local adoption agency. This can provide some useful insight into what the adoptive parents learned and considered in order to make their decisions.

Show your support by making a donation to the loved one's adoption agency or another adoption or child-welfare organization. This is a gracious gesture regardless of whether you still have personal reservations about an adoption.

Help by staying positive for the adoptive parents. Remember that the adoptive parents are probably scared and anxious themselves (no *Horror Stories* required). But continue to learn and to address your own questions and concerns.

Listen. Ask the parents how they're doing. Then listen.

Trust the judgment of your loved ones. They've made the right decisions for themselves and their family.

Look forward to the child that awaits the family—and you.

2

Adoption and loss

My standard public stance on adoption is to sing its praises and share my happy gratitude to be a part of it. I usually prefer to focus on only the most positive aspects of creating or expanding a family through adoption: the option of having a glass of wine (or two) while "expecting;" the memories of my parents meeting my children for the first time; the deep connection to another part of the world adoption can provide; the way it feels when my daughter pulls my arm tightly around her to get even closer when we read together.

But to ignore the hard parts of adoption would be to deny key insights into what the full experience of adoption entails. To really appreciate and understand the experience of your loved ones, you must also be allowed to consider adoption's attendant challenges. Loss is one of them.

In adoption, in order to gain—a child, a family, a parent—there must first be loss. It is a fundamental part of any adoption, and it complicates and deepens the experience of becoming a family in a way that may differentiate adoptive families from other families. Just about anyone involved in an adoption—the adoptive parents, the child, the birth-mother and other birth relatives, and, often, even friends and relatives of the adoptive family—may experience loss as a part of the adoption.

Loss and grief and adoption

Loss and grief related to adoption share qualities with other, perhaps more familiar kinds of loss. One way adoptive parents are taught to think about their adoption-related loss is to consider the classic "five stages of grief" model articulated by psychiatrist Elisabeth Kübler-Ross. (Though the model is most commonly ascribed to loss associated with terminal illness and death, Kübler-Ross saw the model as applicable to any major loss.) Kübler-Ross described those stages as Denial, Anger, Bargaining, Depression, and Acceptance. This model suggests that a person who has experienced a loss must pass through at least two or three of those initial stages in order to accept the loss and thereby move forward. *Not every adoptive parent comes to adoption through grief.* But for those who have, considering those five stages can provide a useful framework for understanding how your loved ones might experience loss and grief as a part of an adoption. Here's one example:

The adoption classes that many prospective adoptive parents take typically include a session in which an adoption educator introduces the concept of loss and its role in adoption. A social worker will suggest that it's likely some of the parents have experienced (and may continue to experience) loss on their path to adoptive parenthood. In my own case, I remember this moment like a light coming on in a dark room. And I wasn't alone in my epiphany. I can still see the other parents around me. No one was doodling or checking their voicemail anymore; all of us were listening very intently to the social worker's words. Here, finally, was a word that explained our complicated experiences and the mixed emotions many of us had felt as we struggled to become parents. *Of course. It's loss. I've experienced loss.*

Once my feelings had been identified, I realized I could begin to deal with them. Until that point, I don't think I really knew what I was wrestling with; I just knew I was struggling. Later, I would be able to identify specific adoption-related losses—my own and that of others. But for now, I could finally see what lay ahead. *You've got to grieve a loss.* And what are the stages of grieving? Denial, anger, bargaining, depression, and acceptance. *So that's why I was angry, then sad, and then ready.*

Some of you, as a friend or family member of the adoptive family, will also have experienced loss as a byproduct of the adoption. You may find you need to mourn this loss before you can be ready to accept and celebrate the child and the adoption. Like anyone else, your loss should be recognized and acknowledged.

The loss of the imagined child

After I married my tall, red-headed husband, my short, basketball-loving mother said, "Now we've finally got a chance for a basketball player in the family." A red-haired, basketball-playing daughter. That's who we anticipated I would produce. We would laugh about it, confident that I could indeed create this very babe, made-to-order to our exact specifications. This is not how things turned out.

A fundamental loss for many adoptive parents is the loss of the "imagined" child. This is the child the parents *thought* they would have: the long-held picture that popped into their minds when they imagined their child—their offspring—as a baby, a toddler, an adult. Part of the assumption of the imagined child is that a parent will have a genetic link to their child. The imagined child has the potential to maintain familiar features and mannerisms. ("I hope he gets Dad's eyes.") The imagined child can carry personal traits into a new generation. ("I hope she gets your sense of direction.") For some, letting go of these expectations and anticipated connections to one's child can be very difficult.

To grieve this loss is critical. Parents must relinquish their ideas about the child they expected to have—and, for some, the way in which they expected to achieve parenthood—in order to be ready to parent their actual child. In my case, in order to make room for my real children, I had to let go of the imaginary red-headed basketball player. She was taking up space that my own kids needed.

This step may be a challenge that other family members share with the adoptive parents. For example, if you are a grandparent, maybe you have been anticipating a mini-replica of your son or daughter. Maybe you've imagined a new but familiar version of yourself or your child, envisioning the child stepping up to bat with the same swing as your son or fitting into an heirloom wedding dress as your daughter did. Other family members—even close friends—may also have expected a particular son or daughter. It's important to acknowledge that you, too, may have lost an imagined child.

Consider the steps of the grieving process, this time as they could apply to you and your own particular experiences and emotions around the adoption. The stages of grieving for a friend or family member of the adoptive parents might look something like this:

Denial: *They're fine. If they just relax they'll get pregnant.*

Bargaining: *I told myself that if my sister could have a child, I would quit smoking.*

Anger: *It's not fair. Why does it have to be so complicated? Other people don't have to go through this.*

Sadness: *I'm sorry my dear friend is hurting. I wish I could give her what she wants and I can't. That's very hard.*

Acceptance: *I want my daughter to be happy. This isn't the child I expected but it's the wonderful child we've received.*

If you find that you need to grieve a loss as part of accepting the adoption, let yourself. You may be able to come to terms with your loss independently or counseling may offer some support. Getting to a point where you can move past the imagined child is important to the real one. It allows them to be appreciated and loved for themselves, unconditionally, as they deserve.

I know, I know. Many of us are used to families that maintain at least a passing similarity among their members. Everyone loves to look for family resemblances: "He's a Fitzpatrick, all right. Look at those blue eyes." "She is the spitting image of you as a baby." "His father was just like him as a boy; always up to something." It feeds our sense of belonging to see familiar traits passed along.

But look at it this way: not all of our family traits may be all that, well, attractive. Maybe it's for the best that no one's bracing themselves for the unfortunate nose from her side of the family. Perhaps it's not a bad thing if someone's tendency toward hysteria ends with this generation. Personally, I'm relieved that I don't have to worry about the appearance of my own weird cowlicks on my children's heads.

However, it's important to recognize that adoption does not have to mean forgoing family resemblances. A child raised in a family of readers is likely to share an appreciation for literature. If Grandma plays piano, and later the child plays piano, it's going to go down in the family history that the child played piano "just like Grandma did." As a prospective adoptive parent, I recall feeling gratified as I listened to an adoptive father and his son describe how they shared an identical goofy sense of humor. It was reassuring to me to realize that a child who was adopted will still embody family traits. And I find that what we perceive to be typical family traits simply evolves: I'm already envisioning future generations of our family as mini-replicas of my children, not of me.

You have an important role to play in helping to ensure

that the child grows up knowing that they are indeed a necessary and integral part of the family: "a Smith" or "a Michaels" or "a D'Angelo." All children need to be assured that they belong, that things are right. It still makes me feel good—secure, even—when people tell me I look like my mother. And as a child, it reassured me that I was right where I was supposed to be. What kid doesn't like to hear that they're an athlete like their aunt or that they share a childhood dislike for vegetables "just like I did." Without denying their uniqueness, children—especially young children—want to know that they fit. You have the authority to tell the child how they're like the rest of the family—so do so. (Do note that it's a common, though well-intentioned, misstep to tell adoptive children or parents that they look like each other when they obviously do not. I've heard several adult transracial adoptees recall childhood confusion at being told things like this when the mirror and their own eyes were telling them something else.)

When you let go of the genetic expectations, you make room for the child's own important contributions to the family. It can be one of those great, unanticipated gifts of adoption. They just get to be who they are. The child deserves this. Of course, any child deserves this.

And the whole family is better for it. Before my eldest daughter came along, no female member of my family had ever gotten anywhere near a pair of jeans bearing the label "lean." And she offers a gentle touch in a family that tends to shove things into place. My son has introduced the most amazing gray eyes into the family photos; and he can fix mechanical problems that leave my eyes crossed. Finally, our youngest arrived with a *joie de vivre* foreign to me and my own occasional tendencies toward Irish melancholy. And—it still makes me shake my head and smile—she's also contributed a whole new shade of red hair with which she brightens the family tree. (We have yet to see her skills on the basketball court.)

Other potential losses of adoptive parents

Depending on their reasons for adopting, your loved ones may also have experienced other adoption-related losses.

Loss of privacy. An unfortunate aspect of adoption is that a lot of people become privy to one's personal life. As a fairly private person, I remember resenting that other people, friends as well as strangers, now had what I saw as evidence of what I'd have preferred to keep a very intimate aspect of my life. Telling people that we were adopting felt sort of like wearing a big scarlet "I" (that's I for Infertile, of course) on my chest. Looking back, I'm sure others weren't nearly as tuned in to in my private drama as I thought they were. But at the time I felt very vulnerable and exposed, and your loved ones may, as well.

Beyond revealing any health issues, the adoption process itself means providing others—again, usually strangers— access to your private life and personal history. Adoption involves mandatory *home studies*—very personal interviews and home visits in which a social worker evaluates the parent and their environment for their fitness for raising a child. Of course, this is a necessary and understandable requirement: the life of a child is involved. Those making the placement must be assured the child is going to a good, safe home. But even though they understand the need for these types of evaluations, a common complaint of adoptive parents is that they have to confront challenges and endure processes that other parents usually don't have to face. One of these challenges is compromised privacy.

Loss of feeling in control. Becoming a parent is a critical, intensely personal point in one's life; it's often a time when a person really wants to be able to move forward on his own terms. That's not possible with adoption, which entails putting a lot of control into the hands of others. Timelines, the child's prenatal care, genetics, the regulations of an adoption agency, a birth country's placement requirements, the conditions of a child's early days or years, the tenuous decisions of other people: these kinds of things are out of one's control.

This aspect of adoption is particularly challenging for those who are used to being able to rely on their own abilities or hard work to make things happen as they wish. I'm one of those people. As my husband and I awaited our first child, I liked to think of myself as "beyond" any issues with pregnancy. And I tried not to compare my situation with others around me who seemed to be easily segueing into pregnancy and parenthood. Instead, I tapped into my tackler's approach to obstacles and diligently set about completing all of the steps necessary to adopt. But I have to admit I found myself more than a little exasperated when a particular young and—by tabloid consensus—irresponsible pop star got pregnant—twice! —while we parenting-manual-reading, thirty-something, rule-followers waited (and waited) for a child. (I believe my exact words were, "Are you kidding me? Again?") I was doing everything right and still couldn't control this aspect of my life. I thought I was annoyed with her, but I was really annoyed with myself and my limitations (and annoyed that I was annoyed).

Prospective adoptive parents can try to regain some control by filling out paperwork as quickly as they receive it, badgering their social workers for updates, and painting and repainting spare bedrooms. But ultimately, one of the big, hard lessons of adoption is that the prospective parents are no longer driving major aspects of their own lives. No doubt the experience is good preparation for parenthood.

Lost concept of oneself as healthy and fertile. For some adoptive parents, one manifestation of loss of feeling in control may be related to their own health. Those who initially came to adoption after first trying to have a biological child may have learned that some aspects of their own health and body are out of their own control. They could not *make* themselves become a biological parent. Some prospective adoptive parents have even had to grieve the very tangible and very difficult loss of a child through miscarriage.

It's common to feel that one's own body has betrayed him or her. If a person is unable to produce a biological child, it may be the first time she or he has not been able to rely on the basic soundness of his or her health. This can even result in new considerations of one's own mortality. There is recognition, perhaps for the first time, that one's own body is vulnerable or imperfect. Those who've faced infertility may need to grieve the loss of their fertility and come to a new understanding of themselves and their bodies in order to proceed with adoption.

Loss and the birthparent

(Note: When discussing birthparents, I reference the example of the birthmother almost exclusively. Of course, both birthfathers and birthmothers—as well as other birth relatives—may be involved in an adoption decision. And any may experience loss as a result. The example of the birthmother should be considered to apply as well to birthfathers and other birth relatives that are aware of and involved in an adoption decision.)

If a child is not orphaned (and the biological parents have not had their parental rights terminated), it is the birth-mother, sometimes in conjunction with a birthfather, who must make the decision to allow someone else to parent her child. This, the birthmother's loss, is central to an adoption. This loss must occur before the adoptive parents can gain a child. Amidst the excitement and anticipation of the child, it can be easy to minimize or ignore this aspect of adoption. But the birthmother's experience of loss is fundamental. Her loss should be recognized and her experience validated.

By considering the perspective of the birthmother and how the adoptive parents regard her, you can begin to understand an important part of the experience of the adoptive parents. Adoption is bittersweet. Though ideally adoption comes as a result of the birthmother making a loving choice for the child, adoptive parents often feel guilty about wanting a child at what can be perceived of as a cost to someone else. Many adoptive parents struggle intensely with the idea that they are benefitting from someone else's loss. They often find themselves balancing their own excitement and anticipation with the concurrent awareness that someone else may be having one of the most challenging and difficult experiences of her life.

Currently, the agency-approved phrasing is to say that a birthmother "makes an adoption plan" for the child. And this term reflects the very deliberate and informed process of decision-making that a birthmother ideally has experienced prior to placing a child with another family. However, though I am certainly a proponent of using thoughtful and careful language around adoption, in this case the less detached description of a woman "giving up" a child for adoption, may also be appropriate. The birthmother, no matter how deeply she is committed to and confident in her adoption decision, gives something up. She is entrusting others—usually strangers—with her child, someone usually deeply precious to her but that she is not in a position to parent. It must require an incredible, unimaginable faith in others—again, strangers even—in order to do this.

The experience of allowing one's child to be adopted entails other residual losses, as well. There is often a loss of privacy: a pregnant woman is on very public display. And a woman who parents a child and later relinquishes it for adoption does not often do so unnoticed. Birthmothers often lack family and societal support for their decision not to parent their child, but to make an adoption plan. A woman will sometimes hide both her pregnancy and her adoption decision (sometimes by leaving home for a time), thus forfeiting the option of family and community support—if indeed it was ever available to her.

Birthmothers live with this loss for the rest of their lives. Anniversaries and holidays—the child's birthday, Mother's Day—are often very difficult. Information about the child and his family (e.g., letters, photos, or other forms of communication) can serve to reassure a birthmother that she made a good decision for her child and may ease the birthmother's grieving to some extent. It's one reason some birthmothers and adoptive families choose to maintain contact.

Expectant adoptive parents are often highly sensitive to the idea that they await someone else's loss in order to gain what they want so much. In order to be parents, someone else has to release—to lose—a child. For these reasons, and this will be addressed further in later chapters, most adoptive parents will speak of birthmothers with respect and gratitude and will appreciate when you do the same. (You can also see *Additional adoption resources* at the end of this book for more information on birthparents and birthparent perspectives on adoption.)

Loss and the child

Ideally, an adoption provides a child with a permanent loving family, a safe and stable home, and opportunities and experiences that might have been otherwise unavailable to the child. These are important, life-long supports that most parents try to provide for their children, and they should not be minimized. But to fully appreciate the adoptive child and his role in the adoption, the consequential sacrifices and losses of the child should be considered as well. To be adopted is to have lost fundamental aspects of one's identity, a privilege that non-adopted people may take for granted. (Open adoptions often offer children access to information around identity and can help to alleviate some of this loss.)

Depending on the age of the child at adoption, he may not understand or identify loss as part of his adoption until he is older. But even for those children adopted as infants, it is possible to feel a sense of loss for something that was never actually possessed but was instead denied them. Because many adoptive children may lack actual memories or a tangible experience with their birth families or cultures, sometimes this loss is referred to as *ambiguous loss*. It's a real loss, even if it may be difficult to identify or articulate.

Some of the losses people who were adopted may experience over time include:

• Loss of a genetic connection to their families, including having a physical resemblance to their family.

• Loss of knowledge of birth culture, possibly including language, customs, history, religion, citizenship.

• Loss of knowledge of biological relatives and family history.

• Loss of other relationships (foster parents, caregivers, friends, etc.).

• Loss of knowledge of one's own health history.

• Loss of control. Children don't "choose" to be adopted—they are too young. Instead, adoption is chosen for them. Some adult adoptees point out that they are the only person in the adoption triad (the birthparent, the adoptive parents, and the child) who did not have a choice in the adoption.

• Loss of a sense of normalcy, of being "like everybody else" in the way they joined a family. Children who were adopted at an older age may feel they've lost the opportunity to have a "normal" childhood.

• Loss of confidence in the stability and security of their family (i.e., fear of future abandonment).

No matter how much she loves her family, no matter how secure she is in her adoption, it's important to recognize that the child has first experienced loss in order to become a part of her family. And it's almost assured that she will at times, to greater or lesser degrees, feel and grieve loss as a result of being a person who was adopted. Many adoptive children and adults have discussed at length and with great insight their experiences of loss and grief related to their adoption. (See *Additional adoption resources* for examples.) It is one of the responsibilities of any parent to try to prepare a child to address and grieve loss in life; adoptive parents must try to help their children grieve loss related to their adoption, as well.

What can you say?

Sometimes, though we may suspect a person has experienced a loss or is facing a challenging time in their life, we avoid broaching the topic with them. Often we're afraid of imposing upon somebody's privacy. Or we don't want to risk drawing attention to a painful topic and risk hurting them anew. Often we just don't know what to say to someone who has suffered an unfamiliar kind of loss.

Depending on your relationship with the adoptive parents, you may wish to acknowledge that loss is a component of your loved ones' adoption. You might do so in very general terms. I don't know that I needed (or wanted) someone to tell me, "I'm sorry you're infertile." (That's a little awkward.) But I did feel comforted when others close to me recognized my experience with words like, "I'm sorry that this hasn't been an easier path for you." Often, I just thanked them and that was the end of the conversation. But the gesture was appreciated and it was enough to make me feel supported by those around me.

If you do say something, I suggest you keep it simple. Express your understanding and recognition that loss is fundamental to adoption. Share your compassion for the potential losses of the child and birthparents, noting your gratitude for them and their roles in this adoption or in adoption in general. You might simply tell the parents more generally that you are thinking about them or sending loving thoughts (or prayers) for those involved in the adoption. These gestures say you recognize that there are important losses to those involved in this experience.

You may decide to acknowledge loss in conversation. You may be more comfortable sending a card or writing a note. You might tell your loved ones that you're reading this book, that it discusses loss, and that it's made you aware of adoption-related losses they and others might experience. You may find less direct ways to demonstrate your understanding and compassion. But if you're close to the parents, consider sharing your insight into this aspect of adoption and of their experience. You can affirm where the family members have been even as you join them in looking forward to what awaits.

Moving forward with loss

Your loved ones have at least begun the process of grieving any adoption-related losses they've had in order to begin making steps toward adoption and parenthood. This doesn't necessarily mean that feelings of loss in connection with the adoption won't recur. Often the experience of mourning a loss isn't finite. Even when parents have grieved their losses and committed to adoption—even when they have the child and want no other child than the exact one they have adopted—adoptive parents may revisit these feelings over time.

One very grateful and devoted adoptive mother told me about how it still bothers her to hear pregnant women complain about their pregnancies. She acknowledges feeling silly about it, but it irks her to hear complaints about a condition that she so tenaciously worked toward and never achieved. Though in a much milder way, these situations still cause her to revisit loss related to her fertility. Some adoptive parents may experience adoption-related grief again in response to major life transitions, as when their own children leave home or become parents themselves.

There's not always a clear and final endpoint to mourning a loss. This potential recurrence of grief is sometimes referred to as cyclical grieving or the *grief loop*, and might be experienced over time by anyone who's had adoption-related loss—including birthparents, children, adoptive parents, relatives and even friends.

As my children know, their father and I want no other children but them. We would happily accept the same challenges (and more) again and again in order to become their parents. Our children are utterly adored and appreciated. So I was surprised to find my eyes filling as I wrote this chapter and revisited my own feelings of adoption-related loss from years ago. But I find that my relationship to these losses has evolved and matured. I am deeply and profoundly grateful that things turned out as they did; and I can see how all of these experiences were necessary in order for me to become my children's mother. I think many adoptive parents, your loved ones included, may recognize themselves in my experience of coming to accept the experience of loss as an integral part of their route to parenthood.

As a friend or relative, an appreciation of your loved one's adoption will likely entail celebrating its benefits: the gain of a niece or a grandchild; discovering a broader concept of family; acquiring a different perspective on humanity. And like any hard-won gain, a child that joins a family through adoption is often uniquely appreciated because of the particular challenges that adoption requires. Recognizing adoption-related losses can further your understanding and appreciation of the privilege that adoption is. But while the experience of loss and grief are integral to adoption, they're also an inescapable part of being a human being. Considered this way, the shared experience of loss in adoption might be a starting point for understanding and compassion among all of its participants— including you—in this utterly human experience.

What you can do

Understand that loss can be experienced by anyone touched by an adoption—child, parents, birthparents, caregivers, relatives, even friends and communities.

Seek to understand the specific ways in which others might experience adoption-related loss. You will likely appreciate even more the great privilege that is adoption.

Validate the experience of your loved ones. Acknowledge what may have been (and still be) a challenging experience for them. Do so directly if you feel it's appropriate. Or consider other ways to indicate your understanding and compassion.

Consider the perspective of the birthparents and their likely experiences of loss.

Consider the perspective of the child who was adopted and her potential experiences of loss.

If necessary, grieve your own adoption-related loss. If you're struggling to move beyond loss, talk with other adoptive relatives and friends. Consider letting a professional help you with the process.

Let others grieve according to their own timeline. Allow others the time and process they may require, though it may differ from your own.

Accept that feelings of loss may recur over time, often unexpectedly. Be open to supporting your loved ones as they may grieve over time.

Celebrate the child's contributions to the family. Reinforce for the child their full and rightful membership in the family, immediately and permanently.

Join the family in looking forward with anticipation. Though loss is fundamental to adoption, so is great gain.

3

The adoption process: Fingerprints, documents, and The Wait

What if adoption worked like it does on television? Babies appear on just the right doorstep. Healthy young birthparents quickly choose the charming, affluent couple for which the audience is rooting, and then disappear (the absence of birthparents being typically depicted as ideal). Cute, well-adjusted toddlers slide easily into new, tastefully decorated lives. In perhaps the breeziest adoption ever, Chandler and Monica wrapped up the final episode of "Friends" with a birthmother producing not one baby but—surprise!—twins (a girl and a boy, naturally). On television, adoption is a quick, straightforward, and clear-cut transaction. No one is too old to adopt from a certain country. No one ever changes their mind at the hospital. No one has health or developmental issues. No grade-schoolers, teenagers, children in foster care, or sibling groups are apparently awaiting adoption. According to these fictional accounts, your ordinary average adoption—from "Let's adopt" to "Here's your [healthy, white] baby"—can be successfully accomplished in one hour of prime time television.

When my husband and I decided to adopt, we thought we were solving a pretty simple equation. Parents want baby. Child needs parents. Child + Parents = Big Happy Family. (As on television, we'd neglected to factor a birth-mother into our early equation.) But as the adoption meetings dragged on, the paperwork piled up, the social worker visited, and the months of waiting passed by, my husband and I were reminded first-hand that real life is rarely as tidy as the televised versions.

People and paperwork

One of the first things prospective adoptive parents learn is that adoption means placing their trust, and the outcome of their efforts to become parents, into the hands of others. Other people will evaluate their fitness for parenthood. Other people will decide whether and when they receive a child. Other people must be trusted to perform their professional duties well and wisely. And even though these "others" are typically compassionate, skilled, and experienced adoption professionals, it still chafes. Adoptive parents embark on a very involved process of meetings and paperwork, evaluation and education. Compared to biological parents, the steps to achieving adoptive parenthood are much more . . . documented.

Every adoption follows its own path, but with variations over time and across states, the following are general outlines of how your loved ones' adoption was (or will be) completed—domestically, internationally, or from foster care.

Steps common to all adoptions—
domestic, international and from foster care

Selection of an adoption agency or attorney. Parents hire either an adoption agency or adoption attorney to manage the adoption process for them and to assist them in finding a child. Parents typically evaluate an agency or attorney based on their own set of criteria or interests. For example, some agencies have a religious affiliation; others have no religious component. Some agencies facilitate international adoptions with various countries; others offer only domestic adoptions. Some parents will be looking specifically for an agency or attorney that provides services for single parents or same-sex parents. The agency or attorney does not have to be in the same state as the adopting family (but must be licensed to practice in that state).

Documentation. Required documents typically include the following: an application to an adoption agency (if using one); mental and physical health histories; background checks; fingerprints; responses to detailed questionnaires covering such areas as the parents' personal values, information about their families of origin, their reasons for adopting, their anticipated parenting styles, etc. Other documentation includes letters of reference; financial records, including income tax statements; housing information and residential histories. These are the materials typically required for an agency adoption to be completed, whether it's domestic, international, or stemming from foster care. Someone working with an adoption attorney—an *independent adoption*—would enter into a contract for legal services.

Adoption education. If parents elect to use an adoption agency, they will typically be required to attend adoption classes or training. (Families not required to attend training may do so anyway.) Some agencies have required reading for families. Classes or reading requirements address such topics as the adoption process itself, potential issues in adoption, understanding loss, and parenting children who were adopted. There are often specific sessions on such topics as becoming a transracial family, foster-to-adopt programs, openness, special needs adoptions, and adopting older children. Panels of adoptive parents or adoptive children will often speak and answer questions for parents. Sometimes birthparents will speak. Parents pursuing international adoptions will receive training around preparing to adopt children from another country and culture. Parents pursuing a domestic infant adoption will learn strategies to connect with birthmothers. Parents interested in adopting *waiting children*—older children in the United States and abroad—receive specific education around those programs. *Many agencies will allow close friends and relatives to attend some of these informational classes, as well.*

The adoption study. A social worker will interview prospective adoptive parents and visit the home in which the child will live. Also known as a *home study*, the social worker's evaluation results in a legal document confirming the safety of the family's home and a prospective parent's capacity to raise a child. It is required for both agency and independent adoptions. In international adoptions, an adoption study is also required by the United States government as a part of the child's immigration and citizenship paperwork.

Financial commitment. Adoption typically requires a significant financial commitment. Fees are paid to the agency or attorney for their professional work facilitating an adoption and for the home study. Fees may also be paid to an organization that has provided a child's care prior to their adoption (There are circumstances in which medical costs and other living expenses during a birthmother's pregnancy may be paid through an attorney or organization, but a woman may *never* legally be paid for a child.). Families often incur travel costs, whether adopting in the United States or abroad. Families also pay costs for documents, notary services, fingerprints, copies, background checks, medical visits, and other professional services (e.g., translations, legal fees, medical document reviews, etc.).

The cost of adoption is a challenge for many families. It can even be a barrier to adoption for some who might otherwise choose adoption. Some families may take out additional mortgages or otherwise go into debt to pay for adoption. Federal tax credits can relieve some of the costs; some employers will also provide support. Adoptions from domestic foster care are typically much less expensive and many (sometimes even all) of the parents' adoption expenses (including fees for a home study and placement) may be covered by the state.

Other steps in a domestic adoption

Following the completion of the general requirements for all adoptions outlined above, additional steps are taken to adopt domestically. (These adoptions usually involve an infant; the adoption of an older child would typically follow foster care).

Meeting a birthmother. In present-day adoptions, the prospective adoptive parents are encouraged to play an active role in identifying a birthmother. To adopt this way, parents need to be willing to share very publicly that they are looking for a child. One adoptive parent called it "marketing herself" to potential birthmothers. This can include placing pages of photos and notes in a physical "waiting families" book reviewed by prospective birthmothers, posting information about themselves in newspapers and online, and otherwise getting the word out that they're looking for a child to adopt. This aspect of domestic adoption can seem very strange, even off-putting, to those who are new to it. ("Seriously? An ad in the Little Nickel?" Yes, and postings on Facebook.) That's how birthparents and families often connect in contemporary adoption.

"Match" meetings. A birthmother, guided by a social worker, reviews potential adoptive parents, often meeting with them in person, to select adoptive parents for her child.

A written agreement. Assisted by a social worker or attorney, adoptive parents and birthparents document expectations for next steps and for contact, both pre- and post-adoption. Both parties can agree to make this a legal document stipulating expectations around contact and communication post-adoption.

A period of legal limbo. Laws vary by state, but there is usually a period, ranging from days to months, in which adoptive parents may have the child under their care, but the adoption is not yet legally final and can be interrupted (i.e., the child could go to a biological parent who still has the right to revoke his or her consent under state law). If it is an interstate adoption (very common), there is often a waiting period during which the adoptive parents have custody of the child in the child's state of birth (usually staying in a hotel), but cannot travel with the child to the parents' home state until both states approve the adoption. Once the stipulated waiting period ends and formal legal documents are signed, the adoptive parents have the right to complete the adoption.

Finalization of the adoption. Assuming all legal requirements were met, the adoptive parents become the legal parents of the child.

Other steps in an international (or *intercountry*) adoption

International adoptions are facilitated through adoption agencies and, because children are typically first made available for adoption within their country of origin, do not typically involve newborns, but older babies and children. After meeting the general requirements for adoption previously described, the steps that follow are typical for an international adoption.

Select and apply to a country. Every "sending" country has its own legal requirements for international adoption. Stipulations as to marital status, age, and health history may limit parents' options for countries from which to choose. (For example, as of this writing, the Chinese government has stipulated that adoptive parents must fall below a set "weight index" and cannot be taking certain medications in order to adopt there.) Adoptive parents compile a *dossier* of legal documents for the sending country, typically including birth and marriage certificates, financial records, photos, health histories, and the agency's home study.

File the required citizenship and immigration paperwork with the U.S. government.

Receive a referral. (Such a dry word for such a life-altering event.) The *referral* is the actual identification of a specific child. It may be a detailed composite or just a photo and a few words. Parents accept or decline the referral.

Acceptance of the child. A legal commitment to adopt the child, signed by the adoptive parents.

Travel to the child's country. Some countries require that parents take more than one trip, one to begin the legal process and another to finalize it. Procedures vary by country, but parents and child are typically united as soon as the parents arrive. They often remain together (staying at hotels especially equipped for adopting families) throughout the time that the in-country legal requirements are being completed. (Sometimes children are escorted from their country of origin to their parents, but this is becoming rare.)

Finalization of legal adoption and citizenship paperwork. Besides finalizing the adoption in the United States, parents adopting children born in another country must take the additional step of documenting the child's new citizenship.

Post-placement requirements. Post-placement reports to the sending country are often required for a set period of time following the adoption (sometimes up to age 18).

Other steps to adopt a child from foster care

Following the completion of the general requirements for adoption previously described, these additional steps are taken to complete an adoption from foster care (the process described is for people who are not already the child's foster parents):

Matching. Following the home study, a *matching* process occurs in which agencies help parents identify children for potential adoption. Some of these children are already legally free to be adopted, i.e., the parental rights of their biological parents have been terminated. Others are not yet legally eligible to be adopted but are anticipated to become candidates for adoption (these children are obviously riskier prospects for potential parents because their eligibility for adoption has not yet been finalized). Children awaiting adoption from foster care are typically older children and teenagers.

Parents may meet with children as well as their prior caregivers, including foster parents and social workers, and possibly including other biological relatives. If all are in favor, *pre-placement meetings* begin to familiarize the potential family members with each other.

Placement. The child is placed in the parents' home. A social worker provides ongoing support to all individuals as they adjust to each other and to their new family. The parents may become temporary foster parents to satisfy the state's requirements for care of the child prior to finalization of the adoption.

Finalization of legal adoption. Assuming all legal requirements were met, the adoptive parents become the legal parents of the child. These are joyous events to which friends and relatives are often invited. If you are invited, go—and bring a camera.

Those are the basic procedures for completing an adoption—domestic, international, or following foster care. However, legal requirements and processes around adoption differ by state and nationality, so expect variation. These are human and very individual situations, so any adoption will depart somehow from the steps described above. But within those process-driven outlines lies one very personal, often nerve-wracking experience common to virtually all adoptive parents: The Wait.

The Wait

As I frequently assure my impatient son, he's right: waiting is hard. And the kind of waiting and patience required for an adoption is a very particular kind of challenge. Rarely is there a fixed schedule or a due date. If the parents have not been matched with an expectant birthmother, they don't have the benefit of the timeline that a typical nine-month gestation period provides. What they do know is that they're waiting for their life to abruptly and completely change . . . at some point. Added to the strangeness and uncertainty of this kind of expectancy, adoptive parents often don't know much about the person or people for whom they're waiting. As a result, an undercurrent of stress and anxiety pervades even the giddiest adopting parent.

Once your loved ones have done all they can to move an adoption process forward—finalized all their paperwork, called their social worker for updates, prepared a room and supplies for the child—all that's left for them to do is wait. Waiting parents know they could get *the call* at any time. So it's hard for them to plan for the future. They don't know if they can move or go to graduate school or even plan a summer vacation. They might have two years until they become parents. Or they might have six weeks. They could get the call tomorrow. The problem is, they don't know which timeline it's going to be—two years or six weeks or tomorrow—and they need to be prepared for all of them.

Added to the absence of a predictable schedule, your loved ones face the more pressing (and exciting) question of who is actually on the way. Like many biological parents, adopting parents often don't know the gender of their coming child. So, again like many biological parents, they may prepare for either a boy or a girl, painting a bedroom a sunny yellow, selecting a green car seat instead of one in pink or baby blue. But unlike biological parents, for adoptive parents, other facts—like the age of the child, and its size upon arrival, even the language the child may have been hearing or speaking—are often unknown. The first time we adopted, I reacted to this uncertainty by buying pajamas in every available size to fit a child—boy or girl—from three months to two years, in styles suited for both summer and winter months. That's a lot of pajamas.

In some adoptions this wait is extended for parents who have received and accepted a referral—sometimes even physically met the child. Legal processes in other countries may require that parents and children wait months or even years after being matched for the adoption to be finalized and for the child to go into the parents' care.

Adoptive parents handle this waiting period in different ways. Many waiting parents, especially if it's their first adoption, say that during this waiting period, they can't believe that the adoption is ever actually going to happen, despite all of the time and effort they've put into it. Many resist fully committing themselves to their future because there's still a great deal of uncertainty. They may hold back their anticipation a little, preparing themselves for the possibility that things might not work out. They may buy little or nothing for the child, afraid to "jinx" the adoption. Or like me, some pass the time by doing everything they can think of to prepare for every possible outcome.

And then it happens. The phone rings. An email arrives. Your loved ones have a new son or daughter. Immediately most adoptive parents decide the whole excruciating wait was worth it—that this is the very person meant to be their son or daughter, and very much worth the wait. (But until it actually happens, is it ever hard to wait.)

As a friend or relative, no doubt this is a time of uncertainty and anticipation for you, too, along with the waiting family.

Waiting friends and relatives

Years after my husband and I adopted our first child, a dear friend recalled how relieved she'd been when we asked her to write one of the letters of recommendation for our home study. She explained that she'd wanted to show us how much she supported us and our adoption plans, but didn't know how to do so. She needed us to suggest some ideas. We had thought we were asking *her* a favor; as it turned out, she was also grateful to *us* for providing her with a way to make a tangible contribution to our adoption.

Most of us have a general idea of how to show our support for an expectant mother who is pregnant. Sure, there will always be those people who touch a pregnant lady's belly without permission or say outrageous things about the woman's size or condition. But most people are familiar with protocols and customs that serve to assure a biological parent that they, too, eagerly await their child. Though some of these ways in

which we might support an expectant biological parent—
accompanying them to doctor appointments, sharing mater-
nity clothes, lamenting their morning sickness—aren't relevant
to parents who are expecting a child via adoption, there are
still plenty of ways for you to be helpful and involved. Following are some ideas, as suggested by adoptive parents.

Help with logistics. Assist with some of the many logistical
components of an adoption. Offer to write a letter of recommendation or track down a parent's birth certificate. Offer
to make copies, mail paperwork, or drop off materials at
the attorney's office. If there are other children in the family, ask if you can care for them while the parents complete
their paperwork and talk through decisions. If you have a
coworker who is adopting, offer support by helping him or
her manage the challenges of planning for a work absence
without a specific due date; let your coworker know they can
depend on you.

Offer to host a shower or party for the expectant parents. Some
parents will want to celebrate before the child arrives, some
after. Some people have welcoming parties following the
adoption in order to introduce the newcomer to friends
and relatives. It's very important to let the adoptive parents
decide this and to respect their decision about it. But either
way, many parents appreciate this kind of public acknowl-
edgement of their new parenthood.

Not only does a shower or party help parents prepare
materially for the child's arrival, but some adoptive parents
appreciate a shower because it provides a chance to, as one

adoptive mother put it, "feel normal" again. Expectant adoptive parents may feel that they miss out on some of the experiences typical of expectant pregnant parents. Participating in a traditional activity like a baby shower can be very affirming for a waiting adoptive parent.

Regardless of when it occurs, an offer of a shower or a party tells the parents that others eagerly await the child as well. One adoptive mother recalled that she'd never been offered a shower for either of her children, adopted 10 and 12 years earlier. In fact, discussing it years later, she was surprised to find that it bothered her still. Looking back, it made her question whether the people around her had supported her choice to adopt.

Show your interest. Ask the adoptive parents if they'd like you to attend any of their adoption classes with them or if you can go on your own. If they are adopting internationally, learn about the child's country of origin. Take the expectant parents out for Ethiopian food or buy them a travel book on China. Collect positive news from that part of the world and discuss it with your friend or relative.

Information-sharing. Waiting adoptive parents are frequently asked "Have you heard anything yet?" Some parents like to be asked if there's news, others gripe that every question is just a reminder that they are still waiting. One way to gauge their attitude about updates is to ask the parents how often they'd like you to check in or how they'd like to share information. This lets them set the pace while also assuring them of your interest and concern.

You might offer to be a main point of contact between the family and other interested friends and family members. Some adoptive parents set up a website or a blog to keep other people apprised of what's going on. This allows them to share new developments—or their frustration at the lack of any—with many people at once. Offer to set this up for them (there are lots of simple templates available online), after which you can help them maintain it or they can update it themselves. It's likely that one day that same website will trumpet an adoption announcement.

Financial support. Adoption is often expensive. Though some parents will not accept it (and that's okay), a *graciously offered* monetary gift or an offer to donate air miles is another way to support the family and the adoption. Some people help by leading fundraising efforts for the family (but be sure to get the parents' approval before doing any fundraising on their behalf). One adoptive family was very pleased to receive plane tickets as a Christmas gift from their extended family the year they were expecting to travel to their first child. They called it a "wonderful, wonderful memory" from their time of expectancy.

Help for traveling families. In both domestic and international adoptions, many parents travel to meet their new child. Before they travel, help them with packing and shopping. Offer to provide rides to and from the airport (and plan ahead to have a baby seat or booster chair ready for the return trip). If they're traveling with older children, send along activities—art supplies, workbooks, games—to occupy their time on long flights and in hotels.

Offer to keep the household running when they're traveling: collect mail, pay bills, water plants, mow the grass or shovel snow, care for pets, etc. While they're gone, be sure to keep in touch by email or via their blog if they have one. Parents who adopted outside their own immediate community told me repeatedly how important those messages were to them when they were far away from friends and family at a time when their lives were changing dramatically.

Both domestic and international adoptions may require a lengthy hotel stay while legal issues (like waiting periods) are resolved. One adoptive parent noted that, "It's no fun to care for a child in a hotel room" and suggested that some loved ones might offer to travel with the parents to help. Don't be offended if they decline your offer; often parents prefer to spend this early time as a new family alone. If you do offer to travel, be sure you are truly able to be helpful. One parent found herself caring for both her new child and her mother over several exhausting weeks in an overseas hotel. Her mother, though with the best of intentions, had never before traveled internationally. She found herself overwhelmed and more dependent than was helpful to her daughter, the new mom.

Before the family returns, fill their refrigerator with some basic supplies and meals to save them an immediate trip to the grocery store. Pick up diapers and formula if appropriate (ask about sizes and brands). Offer to make any appointments they may need soon after their return.

If the family is adopting internationally, try to respect the sending country's adoption process. Every government devises its

own procedures by which intercountry adoptions are completed, working toward the goal of ensuring that every adoption is safe, ethical, legal, and conducted in the best interests
of the child. Not every country moves with the same effi-
ciencies that those of us from Western countries may expect.
It's important that others try to respect each country's right
to devise and implement its own procedures.

Some governments require that adoptive parents remain
in their child's country of origin as the legal process is
completed, often a protracted stay. Several adoptive parents
whose adoptions required long stays in the sending country
remarked that it was offensive when others criticized their
child's birthplace, suggesting, for example, that the country
required a long stay to "make money off of foreigners." In
fact, many families appreciate that time as an opportunity to
both become familiar with their child's birth country and to
spend time alone as a new family.

Help with other children. If there are other children in the
waiting adoptive family, try to include and acknowledge
them and their experience, as well. Older siblings typically
feel at least a little threatened by a new child joining the
family, resenting the changes in their lives that result. The
excitement and novelty of adoption can be an added challenge for a waiting sibling. And the wait itself is stressful
for many kids. Remind the sibling of how uniquely special
it was when he arrived or was born; use this opportunity
to retell the story of how his family once awaited him, too.
Buy him a t-shirt that trumpets his new role ("I'm the big

brother"). One aunt sent her niece a box of "big sister" presents to open daily during the trip to adopt her sibling. Reassure the older child of how special she is, whether an adoptive or biological child. Make plans to spend time alone with the sibling when the new child arrives.

Normalize their experience. Treat your loved ones like any other expectant parents. Make snarky comments like "Enjoy eating in nice restaurants now because that's gonna change!" Offer to share equipment or clothing. Compile a list of potential babysitters. Make a list of things to do with kids: good playgrounds, kid-friendly restaurants, group music classes, etc. (This kind of information is especially helpful for new parents of older children; they may find themselves suddenly immersed in a kid-centered world, but with little knowledge of the resources and options for children within their community.) Debate the merits of educational TV for toddlers and ask if they've started their child's college fund.

A secondary but important reason to ask questions and make suggestions about parenthood is because your questions and suggestions show you have faith in the adoption. One adoptive parent recalls appreciating how some people would preface questions with "when you have kids" instead of "if you have kids." Small gestures like the ones described above reassure the waiting parents that other people also believe that one day, after all of the obstacles and challenges have been overcome, after all the waiting and worrying, they will indeed actually be done with the process of *becoming* a parent and actually get to *be* one.

What you can do

Offer to help with logistics. Many adopting families will welcome the help of an amateur executive assistant: copy paperwork, make deliveries, track down records.

Offer to host a shower or welcoming party for the new child. Allow the adoptive family to stipulate timing—or decline altogether.

Show your interest. Become an informed enthusiast of their adoption and impending parenthood.

Facilitate information-sharing for the family. Try to gauge how often to ask for updates. Offer to be an intermediary for sharing with others.

Consider offering financial support. Fundraising or other material support (clothing, equipment, furniture, air miles) may also be welcome.

Assist traveling families. Help with transportation, offer to maintain the household while they're traveling, or prepare their home for their return.

Help with siblings. Offer to babysit while the parents do adoption-related tasks. Pay extra attention to waiting siblings.

Treat them like the excited expectant parents they are.

4

Digging deeper: Beyond the paperwork

I'm a lady who likes to tackle a To Do list. Give me an inventory of items to pick up at the hardware store, a recipe to follow, or assembly instructions for a piece of furniture and I will eagerly produce a bag of hardware, a (fairly) well-made dish, or a set of shelves for the kids' playroom. So for me, the physical adoption process, while cumbersome, was really just another checklist challenge to be met. Fingerprints notarized? Done. Copies made? Done. Called my social worker? Emailed my social worker? Otherwise nudged my social worker? Done, done and done.

But preparing for adoption required much more of me than simply ticking off tasks on a checklist (though there's plenty of that). More will be required of your loved ones, as well. This chapter addresses some of the deeper, more intimate and consequential preparations your loved ones made in their adoption process, beyond the meetings and the compilation of paperwork. These steps may have included preparing for openness in their adoption, preparing for the unique responsibilities of parenting transracially, or preparing to meet the particular needs of older children in adoption. Having some familiarity with some of these key factors in contemporary adoption—and some suggestions as to how your loved ones may address them—will be helpful to you.

Honesty and access

Not so long ago, adoption records were sealed and legally inaccessible, even to adult adoptees seeking their own information. In fact, sometimes people were never even told they were adopted. Names and birth certificates were changed to read as though the child's adoption were her life's starting point, ignoring—even erasing—the child's prior history. The practice of adoption generally mandated that it was best that there be no contact with the birthparent, either by the adoptive parents or the child. And often, little if any information about the child's personal history was shared between the birthparent and the adoptive parent, including genetic history.

Over time, this emphasis on secrecy—to the point of an inability to access one's own personal history—came to be seen as detrimental to everyone involved in an adoption, particularly to the adopted child.

The fact of an adoption is now virtually never kept a secret. Today, most children who were adopted always know they were adopted, from their very earliest understanding of themselves. It's likely that the child adopted by your loved one will never remember being told they were adopted. There's usually no big announcement; rather it's an acknowledged part of a child's identity even before she can truly understand its meaning. And the child's right to have access to her personal information is a foundational value of contemporary adoption practice. (Unfortunately, these changes are not necessarily retroactive; even as contemporary adoptees benefit from an approach that idealizes access to one's own information, many older adoptees are still legally unable to access their own adoption records.)

Open adoptions

As previously noted, a critical factor with which your loved ones must come to terms is the existence of a birthmother (and sometimes a birthfather or other biological relatives). In the past, a birthmother might have been a young woman who "went away" for several months and then quietly returned to her community amid whispers and rumors. The word *birthmother* might conjure for you the image of a young woman, in a different and poorer country, leaving a baby to be found and cared for by others, forever anonymous herself. I will admit that I had a very *After School Special* idea of birthmothers. I pictured a middle-class suburban teenager, dumped by her boyfriend, hiding her growing belly from her parents until she no longer could. Drama ensued, the baby was adopted by some nice, faceless family, and the young woman headed off to finish high school without a backward glance.

All of these birthmother stereotypes have this in common: the birthmother's role in the adoption—and in the child's life—ended with the birth of the child. This approach was once considered best for everyone involved in the adoption. But perspectives on the role of the birthmother in the life of the adoptive family have shifted over the years. Adoption practitioners now advocate for openness, defined simply as some degree of communication between the adoptive family and the birthmother.

Openness means something different in every situation. Some birthmothers want no ongoing contact with the adoptive parents and child but provide detailed personal and health information prior to the adoption. Birthparents and adoptive parents may negotiate infrequent and fairly detached contact, sometimes using an agency or social worker as intermediary and limiting access to specific private information (last names, direct contact information, etc.). Other open adoption relationships involve quite personal and regular contact. Like any relationship, these evolve over time. And the level of contact that parents think they want *before* an adoption is typically quite different than what they find they want *after* the adoption (when they often find they'd prefer more opportunities for information and communication). If your loved ones have an open adoption, their early plans for how openness will work in their family may look nothing like what the relationship ultimately becomes.

The greatest perceived value to the practice of openness has to do with how information about one's personal history can benefit the child. Initially, contact—even via intermediaries—can provide useful health and genetic histories for the child and parents. Later, contact can offer the child a resource for answers to questions around identity and self. The option to know and understand the reasons for their adoption is often precious to people who were adopted. Having this information, though it is sometimes very, very hard, can help adoptive children as they grieve their own adoption-related losses. And openness may eventually provide adoptive children with the opportunity for a relationship with a birthmother or other members of their birth families. Just having these choices—for more information or for contact—is often deeply valuable and reassuring to people who were adopted, whether or not they ever choose to pursue them.

Besides benefitting their children, your loved ones may value openness in adoption out of feelings of compassion for the birthmother. Having information about the adoptive child can help a birthparent as she grieves the loss of her child. Knowing that the child is growing up in a family that loves and cares for him can provide reassurance that her adoption decision was the right one for herself and the child.

Of course, not every birthmother has the option to receive information about her child and his adoptive family. Systems for adoption vary worldwide, and policies regarding the practice of openness vary, as well. In intercountry adoption, for example, government or social service agencies typically act as coordinators; the birthmother's active role often ends when she relinquishes the child to intermediaries.

Such adoptions are often conducted in relative anonymity—much as they once were in the United States—and there is often little or no information provided to the adoptive family about the birthparents or to the birthparent regarding the adoptive family. Thus there may be few avenues for future communication available to any of the parties involved. Though it is true that some parents choose to adopt internationally in part because of the diminished role of the birthparent following the birth of the child, some parents of internationally adopted children come to lament the limits to information and future communication typical of this type of adoption.

Just like many adoptive parents, as a friend or relative, your initial reaction to the concept of openness may be resistance; this likely stems directly from valid feelings of protectiveness and concern for the adoptive family. And many adoptive parents do choose more closed adoptions with no or very limited contact. But whether or not birthparent contact is a part of your loved one's adoption, it is one of the major issues they had to consider during their preparation to adopt.

Transracial adoption

If your loved ones attended adoption classes as part of their adoption process, it's likely they received some preparation for creating an interracial family and for raising children of a race other than their own. Interracial families are very, very common in adoption. Currently, the majority of transracial adoptions by American parents (domestic or international) comprise white parents and children of color. But the realities and challenges of transracial adoption will affect any transracial adoptive family, regardless of its composition.

Adoptive parents learn that to simply love their children who are of a race other than their own—and they will, profoundly—does not fulfill their obligations to the child. Indeed they have an added responsibility to try to prepare their children for a world that will sometimes treat them in ways that are race-based, an experience that may be unfamiliar to the parents. This reality can be challenging for Caucasian parents, who have typically lived as part of a majority culture, to identify and understand on behalf of their children.

I once heard a young adult adoptee, ethnically Hispanic, describe "the umbrella" of his otherwise Caucasian family. He said that when he was "under the umbrella" of his family—when he was with them or when people knew of him or his family—he was treated just like the other members of his family (i.e., as familiar, even as "white"). But when he was away from his family and among strangers, he was treated as a young Hispanic man, differently—and sometimes more poorly—than when under the Caucasian umbrella. His point was that children of color, though raised in an interracial family, will have experiences based on their race that their Caucasian parents have not. If your loved ones adopt transracially, they are asked to recognize a responsibility to try to understand this, to accept it, and to do what they can to help to prepare their children for these experiences.

Because they are being raised by parents of another race does not make these children exceptions to their own race. In contemporary adoption, parents are advised to acknowledge and support the child's racial heritage, rather than to ignore it (an approach once advocated as a means to best assimilate a child of another race into a family). Adoptive parents are encouraged to provide their children access to people of their own race and to provide experiences that help children explore and connect with their racial identity. So, for example, race might be one factor your loved ones consider in selecting a doctor or a childcare provider. They might include art and music in their homes that reflects the various races and origins of the people that reside there. They might vacation and dine in places that allow the children to hear their native language spoken. Interracial families—adoptive or not—often consider race when making certain choices for their children—from the toys and books they bring home to the daycares and schools the children attend. Some families move to communities and neighborhoods that better reflect and support the racial diversity of their own family. Of course, these values are not exclusive to interracial or even adoptive families; plenty of same-race, biological families hold these values, as well.

There are voices in the adoption community itself—some quite compelling—that advocate for children being raised only in families of their own race or country of origin. Members of this group include some adult adoptees who were themselves adopted into families of another race or nationality. Some of these adoptees articulate acute resentment at being removed from a culture or community in which they would have been in the norm and instead raised in an environment in which they were usually the exception. I've even heard adoption equated to "kidnapping," in that the child often has no choice about his adoption and, is in fact adopted (taken) against his will (an extreme interpretation, to be sure). In 1972, the National Association of Black Social Workers even advocated that only black parents should parent black children, resulting in black children who might otherwise have been adopted being raised in foster care rather than by non-black parents (importantly, this is no longer the Association's position).

Despite their own willingness to adopt across races or nationalities, your loved ones may encounter dissenting voices not only within their own circles but within those communities from which they would adopt. These are not the prevailing perspectives, but they are opinions adoptive parents may hear. Ultimately, most people, across races, determine that having a family is more important for a child than racial homogeneity within that family.

Though the adoptive parents may have committed to adopting transracially, it is an aspect of adoption that may initially make some friends and relatives of the family uncomfortable. Sometimes the already unfamiliar practice of adoption is only compounded by adding a family member of a different race. And some people may have reservations about their own capacity to develop a relationship with a child of another race.

Remember, if your loved ones adopt transracially, they will likely have considered the family and community in which their child will be raised and weighed the impact of the child on their family—and that of the family and community on the child. One Caucasian adoptive parent described how she considered her capacity to parent a child of another race and decided that she could provide support for the child's racial identity, both by her own willingness to address it and using the resources of her community. However, she recalled having great anxiety about introducing her father to her baby. Growing up in a small, homogenous community, she'd had experiences that caused her to be concerned that her father wouldn't welcome a child of another race. She remembers having decided to adopt transracially "despite" her low expectations for her father's response. Instead, she was delighted and gratified by the sight of him proudly cradling the child as he showed off his granddaughter to others. Someone unfamiliar had become beloved.

The experiences and voices of adults who were transracially adopted are now being heard. They are informing the adoption community's understanding of best practices in transracial adoption and affecting how many new adoptive parents approach this aspect of parenting. And these adult adoptees suggest some ways that others, as a friends or relatives of a transracial adoptive family, can help to integrate the child into the family and community.

One well-intentioned approach to welcoming a child of another race is to take the position that the child is "no different" from the rest of the family or community. People may say things like, "We don't see her as African-American [or Asian or Hispanic]. We don't see color. She's just part of our family." Though likely meant to be inclusive, this approach may have another, albeit unintended, consequence.

Adult adoptees speak of how ignoring the fact of their inherent differences, in this case their race, ignores and even devalues a critical part of who they are. And ignoring racial differences invalidates or negates what they themselves may experience—outside of the "umbrella" of their family. An Asian-born child may be a cherished member of an otherwise Caucasian family that fully embraces her, but outside of her family she will at times be treated as "other": not only "other than Caucasian" but also "other than Asian," depending on the person, the circumstances, the environment.

Within our families, we know our loved ones as so much more than their race. But that doesn't mean that racial differences can simply be dismissed. It is an important aspect of our loved ones, among many important aspects. One adoptive mother encourages her friends and family to "feel comfortable recognizing my child's race and birth culture instead of being colorblind." It's important that the child's own experiences and racial identity, separate from that of his family, be valued and affirmed.

This doesn't just benefit the child. One of the great privileges of adoption, particularly transracial adoption, is that it offers all of its participants opportunities to broaden their understanding of other people's life experiences and to connect with people and communities they might not otherwise. If you are related to a family that has adopted transracially, you are now a part of an interracial family, too. I have learned that most adoptive parents and their loved ones find that adoption—transracial or not—can focus and deepen their very connection to humanity, across races, and that this is another unanticipated gift that a child may bring to the family.

Adopting older children

Adoptions of newborn infants are now the exception. Many adoptions involve older children—from several years old to teenagers. Adoptive parents of older children not only face unique issues in adoption but will likely face them immediately. As one mother of Russian-born girls adopted at ages one and four put it: "Parenting an older adopted child is not the same as parenting a biological child or a child adopted as an infant. Period." Following are some of the particular issues that parents adopting older children may have to addresss.

Forming attachment. Building attachment and creating trust among immediate family members is paramount in adoptions of older children. Working to make the essential connections between parent and child (and siblings if they're involved) is a deliberate process; the adoptive parents usually won't just rely on time and affection to draw the family together. Rather, they will pursue specific, conscientious strategies to do so. Consider that an older child will often have had several caregivers (versus a single primary caregiver) prior to his adoptive parents. The child may no longer trust that connections will last; he may have learned to always be looking for his next caregiver. It is essential that the child begin identifying his adoptive parents as his primary and permanent caregivers.

To achieve this, your loved ones may do things like require that they be the only people to provide direct care to the child. They may ask, for example, that no one but a parent feed or diaper the child. One adoptive mother described asking her mother repeatedly not to feed her child directly, telling her "a potato chip is not always just a potato chip." A further complication occurred when the grandmother then challenged the mother about this approach in front of the child. The grandmother may have been used to a conversation style that involved casually (and publicly) arguing with her daughter over minor issues. But now the adoptive mother needed her newly-arrived child to see her—the child's new mother—as having final authority in the home. Understand that actions or words that might otherwise seem innocuous or unremarkable can cause unintended harm when they involve a new adoptive family immersed in the critical process of securing attachment.

Securing attachment with a child who has experienced abandonment or trauma or who has had little constancy in their past can be complicated. It's important that the people around the new family understand that this is critical work for the family. Some families "cocoon" for months, getting to know each other and building the base for their lifelong parent-child connection before they begin expanding the child's circle of visitors and caregivers. Often, other relationships must come second to this process.

Friends and family may find these boundaries confusing or unreasonable. After all, you, too, have been waiting for the child and are eager to begin knowing him. If parents set up systems or limits that don't make sense to you or with which you don't agree, ask them to help you understand them. It's likely they have information and insights that will reassure you.

Standards for behavior. If a child has been adopted after inadequate care or following trauma, several parents strongly recommended that others not expect typical maturity or behavior from these children. One adoptive parent recalled needing to respond to a friend's comment about her daughter's behavior ("an eight-year-old shouldn't be doing that anymore"). From her adoption preparation, the parent knew that sometimes, depending on the level of care a child received prior to their adoption, the child's chronological age may not match their developmental age. The mother had a unique set of expectations for her child based on this knowledge. She explained this to her friend, who hadn't before considered a child's development this way and who immediately understood the need for an unconventional approach.

Like the parents, those who want to support the family may have to adjust their expectations for what constitutes acceptable behavior for that child. These children may react to situations or environments differently—often more intensely—than other children. One father said, "We learn to pick our battles, and others think we are being too easy on them." Parents spoke of feeling abandoned or judged by people, including friends and relatives, whose expectations for their children were unreasonable, considering the children's extraordinary backgrounds.

Whether or not you agree with your loved ones' approach

to parenting their child, try to respect it. One adoptive parent put it this way: "You may have been a parent, but if you've never parented a child from another country, or from another culture, who arrives speaking another language, and has been traumatized, you don't know how to parent *this* child. Please don't judge." Another parent offered this advice: If a parent who has adopted older children asks you to avoid certain things with regard to the child (e.g., certain situations, behaviors, etc.), please listen to them. The parent may not be able to explain why (sometimes just for simple lack of energy but perhaps also to maintain the child's privacy), but know they are asking for a reason.

Adoptive parents of older children advise that, at the very least, it's important to withhold comment in front of the child, demonstrating support for the parents in front of the child, no matter what you really think. The child needs to know that the parents are consistent and reliable forces in their lives and that the parents' decisions are final.

If your loved ones adopt older children or children who've experienced trauma, you can be very helpful to them simply by supporting the attachment process and taking care to do nothing to interrupt it. Help with permanency by keeping any commitments you make to the parents or the child— promises are always serious to a child, but even more so to one who needs to begin trusting in the consistency of others. One adoptive parent suggested that others offer to give the parents a break by staying with the child at night or while she's napping, thus allowing the parents a break while not confusing the identity of caregiver. You may be helping in ways different than you expected, different than the ways in which you've helped other new families, but trust that there are many, many ways to support your loved ones who've adopted older children. Ask what you can do; ask how you can help.

The new family

Again, learning about adoption and about being an adoptive family will likely be an ongoing process for both you and your loved ones. Beliefs about best practices will change, the experiences of older adoptive families will continue to inform new families, and societies and norms will evolve. But in the meantime, a child has joined the family (or will soon). In any new family, when the child arrives, the parents will appreciate your participation, your assistance and your continued support. Following are some suggestions for helping the new adoptive family.

Let the parents determine how and when to introduce the child to others. The parents will try to ensure a transition that is as smooth as possible for their child, who is encountering many new people in unfamiliar surroundings. (This is important for both babies and older children.) One parent noted that an airport surprise party of 100 people was not good timing for the tired adopting family and in particular for the bewildered child. Instead, ask when the family would like to see you, and allow them to set the timeline. Remember that it's very common for adoptive parents to ask that friends and relatives provide the new family with some room to adjust after the child arrives in the home. One said, "Please don't be offended if the family needs 'just family' time to bond. Attachment is *very* important with the core family right now." Some families just need to cocoon for a while. But do ask. I cherish the memories of entering the baggage claim area of our airport, knowing I would find a small group of close family eagerly waiting to welcome their newest member.

Treat them like you would any new family. Bring them a meal. Take family photos for them. Check in by phone and email. Give them a gift certificate for take-out or a pedicure. Join them on a walk or take the parents out at night—any parent appreciates time with other adults, even if it's just an opportunity to see an unanimated movie.

Gifts. Gift-giving is a thoughtful, tangible way that we welcome a child's arrival into a family. When you have a choice, consider selecting gifts that reflect or include the child's racial or ethnic heritage (e.g., books, toys). When we wanted to populate our daughter's new dollhouse, we bought two sets of families—one brown-skinned, one fair-skinned—and mixed all of the dolls together in one box so that our daughter's dollhouse would feature a family that resembled her own. One adoptive mother told me how her "very boy-oriented" seven-year-old son, a "LEGO, Star Wars, Indiana Jones, collector car fanatic" asked his grandmother for a certain American Girl doll for his birthday, one with African-American features similar to his own. He wanted to have another face like his own in his home. His mother described how, after receiving the doll, he paraded it around his house, saying happily, again and again, that it looked just like him.

If you have any question as to whether a gift is appropriate, do ask the parents. Sometimes even very thoughtful gifts may have unintended consequences. The mother of Russian-born daughters described one daughter's response when a well-intentioned relative, as a surprise for the family, played them a CD of Russian music. Hearing music she associated with her past life was very upsetting for the girl; "it sent her into an emotional tailspin." Things like music and food and smells can evoke powerful responses, so always check with the parents first.

Let them complain. Whiny gradeschoolers, late night feedings, toddler tantrums: at various times, any parent finds parenthood hard, boring, frustrating, exhausting, and mundane. Sometimes adoptive parents feel particularly guilty about acknowledging these feelings because they worked so hard—so publicly hard—to become parents. They may worry about seeming ungrateful about something for which they are, of course, deeply grateful. Reassure them that their feelings are normal. One adoptive parent put it this way: "I would have liked the people around me to assure me that it's ok—that the first year is a real transition. It's ok to worry that you made a mistake. You don't know what to do. You don't know who you are anymore. You want your old life back. You're not a bad adoptive parent if you have those feelings. Every parent thinks that. You don't love your child any less." Let them know that these are the experiences and emotions of a new parent, any new parent, and not wrong.

Watch for depression and anxiety. Several adoptive parents advised watching for signs of post-adoption depression in new parents. Like post-partum depression, post-adoption depression can follow the arrival of a child. As with all new parents, the lives of new adoptive parents have changed dramatically. They may be stressed, jetlagged, exhausted and anxious. The very public experience and anticipation of adoption may make parents hesitant to seek help if they're overwhelmed. And adoptive parents may question the validity of their own feelings because they've not experienced the pregnancy associated with post-partum depression.

Remind them—or inform them, because they may not have been made aware of it—that depression following an adoption is not unusual and can be helped. Skilled support is available, both from therapeutic professionals and within the adoption community. (For more on post-adoption depression or PAD, see *Additional adoption resources* at the end of the book.)

Provide respite. This is one of the best ways to help any family. As one adoptive father put it, "There is nothing more wonderful than hearing a parent or friend say, 'Can I give you a hand or take the kids to a movie so you can have a break?' Those moments are so helpful for parents, allowing them space to regroup and reenergize." A single adoptive parent suggested that friends and relatives "remember the parent is on duty from start to finish—with additional midnight responsibilities for water breaks and nightmares. A break from childcare makes us all better parents."

Enjoy. There is so much joy to be found amidst the tumult of a new family and a lot of fun to be had. Relish it.

What you can do

Seek to understand the adoption process that occurs beyond the paperwork. Respect the particular kinds of knowledge and experience your loved ones have acquired while adopting and how this may impact their approach to parenting.

Consider the value of information and communication in an adoption. Understand the continuum of openness and the importance of access to information, particularly for the adoptive child.

Examine the issues involved in transracial adoption. Consider how you can work to support a family that has adopted transracially.

If your loved ones have adopted an older child, help them as they make securing attachment within the family their paramount concern. Follow their lead.

Let your loved ones decide when and how to introduce the child to those outside the immediate family.

Treat them as you would other new parents. Bring gifts, provide respite, let the parents complain a little, look for signs of stress or depression, offer help, enjoy the new family.

5

Welcoming the whole child: Personal histories

C hildren awaiting adoption don't drop from a stork.
They don't pop up from a cabbage patch. They rarely
arrive via airplane and escorted by a social worker any
more. These children are from somewhere and from someone. They arrive at their families bringing with them that
which is their own: their genetic backgrounds, their experiences—remembered or not—and their personal histories:
the people, the cultures, the circumstances, and the decisions
that made them available for adoption. Welcoming a child
who was adopted means welcoming the whole child, and all
that accompanies her, to her family.

Birthmothers

*(Note: Again, while acknowledging that birthfathers and other
birth relatives may also have a role in an adoption, I will primar-
ily reference birthmothers. The example of the birthmother should
be considered to apply as well to birthfathers and birth relatives
that are aware of and involved in an adoption decision.)*

The most significant element of an adoptive child's personal history may be the very fact of a birthmother. Many adoptive families seek to hold the birthmother in high regard, and for reasons even beyond her pivotal decision to place the child for adoption. She is the person who created this child. She gave her child life and physical characteristics and personality traits. Most adoptive families recognize that the birthmother has an *ongoing* place in their families; this is true even for those women who remain unknown or unreachable.

By relinquishing her child, this woman allowed your loved ones to become the child's parents. To a greater or lesser degree, she arrived with her child—she is part of the child. Regardless of what the adoptive parents do or do not know about the birthmother, and what level of contact they have or desire with her, it is likely important to them that she be considered with respect and compassion.

A friend and fellow adoptive mother describes how her father, a deeply devoted and doting grandfather, used to say, while gazing upon his granddaughter, "I don't see how anyone could ever give you up." With these words he was saying, "I love this little girl so much. She is precious to me and I will protect her from need or harm. I will take care of her forever—I'd never give her up and I don't understand how anyone else could." These are loving thoughts. So why did his daughter suggest to him that his words were disrespectful of the birthmother, someone they wanted their daughter to know is deeply respected by her parents?

The grandfather's words were meant to convey his great

love for the child, but they sent another message, as well. Though unintended, his question disparaged the birthmother by asking, basically, "What kind of person could give you up?" It's that implied "what kind of person" that demeans the birthmother; it's like saying a good person, an honorable person would not "give up" a baby. This mother felt that her father was inadvertently suggesting to her daughter that her birthmother was someone of lesser value than they. This family did not at all view the birthmother as inferior to themselves. And a child should never be embarrassed or ashamed of her background, including her birthmother.

"Adoption is an act of love." It's a billboard-worthy phrase that adoptive parents see again and again, so much so that, at least in my case, I started to see it mechanically, without really internalizing the words. So, if I heard someone say, "Adoption is an act of love," my early reaction was pretty much along the lines of, "Well, that's obvious. We parents are going to adopt a child and love him. That's the act of love." I now realize that I had a very immature understanding of those words. The act of adopting (and then parenting) our children is indeed an act of great love. But another essential, inciting act of love underlies many adoptions. That is the birthmother's decision to allow others to parent the child.

There are so many reasons that a woman might relinquish a child for adoption. She may be unable to care for any child (or another child) at that time in her life, perhaps lacking the financial, physical, personal, and/or legal ability to do so. She may be without the family and community support and resources that might otherwise help her raise her child. In fact, she may feel she had no real choice as to whether to parent her child—that relinquishment was a forced necessity.

A benefit of open adoptions is that they can provide an opportunity for the birthmother to share with the adoptive family and her child her reasoning and emotions around the adoption. Many birthmothers articulate their deep and abiding love for their child, the intense difficulty of making their decision to relinquish the child, and their hopes for their child's future with their adoptive families. But even in adoptions for which there is no information about or contact with the birthmother, evidence of her love and regard for the child can often be found. It can be an act of love to carry a baby for nine months, oftentimes in an environment lacking support, one of judgment or secrecy. It can be an act of love to recognize that you are not able to raise that child well but that someone else could. It can be an act of love to make contact with an agency that will care for the child and find parents for the child. It can be an act of love to try to parent a child and to ultimately decide that another home would be better for the child. And it can be an act of love to leave a baby in a safe place and know that she will be found and cared for.

These may not be acts we most immediately associate with showing one's love for a child. And sometimes the circumstances under which a child becomes available for adoption do not in any way demonstrate someone's care or concern for the child. But it benefits the child and the rest of the adoptive family when the adoption and its circumstances can be *truthfully* understood as a thoughtful, caring act—even an act of love—on the part of the birthmother.

The birthmother has this essential role in the child's life. It's both an obvious aspect of an adoption, and a deeply personal and intimate aspect of it. Within the family, the topic of the birthmother is often highly sensitive and handled with great care and intention. It's a subject that should most likely only be broached by a member of the immediate adoptive family. Friends and relatives of the adoptive family should think very hard about whether and how to ever discuss this piece of a child's personal history. If you do discuss the child's birthmother (or birthmothers in general), try to do so with gratitude and respect. At the very least, strive to remain neutral and to resist voicing judgment of these women. Remember that the birthmother (and any other birth relatives) is a part of the child. Others' perspectives on her can affect the child's perception of himself.

Birth cultures and countries

Another important part of a child's personal history is her birth culture or country of origin. Accompanying the child to her adoptive family may be things like a cultural history (e.g., religion, language, and customs), typical physical characteristics, or a genetic predisposition for certain health conditions. And whether domestic or international, the child's original environment contains its own history and cultural norms, and its own circumstances that result in the availability of children awaiting adoption. This is all part of what the child brings with her to the family.

If a child is adopted internationally, a critical factor in a child's adoption has to do with the birth country's policies and practices around adoption. One hallmark of a well-functioning society is its ability to care for its children. Most countries, including the United States, strive first to place adoptable children within their own borders and among fellow citizens. No country wants to have to look to adoptive parents from other countries to help them do so. Yet consider the ramifications for children when countries and societies cannot adequately care for them and yet do not allow foreign adoptions. This happens, too.

My own children were adopted internationally. I know that the country in which they were born valued them because it reaches beyond its borders to find parents for children who would otherwise not have permanent families. The government's policies and procedures ensured my children had a safe environment until their parents—ones from outside the country—could take over their care. Though no country takes pride in having to find parents for its children outside of its borders, many do it anyway (including the United States), resulting in tens of thousands of international adoptions every year.

International adoption:
the family's connection to their child's birth country
Because they love their child—their whole child—an international adoptive family will have, at some level, a

relationship with their child's country of origin. I've come to appreciate and value what will be a lifelong relationship with my children's birth country. If your loved ones adopt internationally, it's likely they will have this relationship, as well.

My children were born in Colombia, a country that takes pride in preserving its ancient architecture and the artifacts of early civilizations even as its urban areas provide contemporary models for transportation and development initiatives worldwide. It's a country that produces artists recognized globally for their contributions to literature, music, and the visual arts. In Colombia, children and family are highly valued, and people tend to be educated, welcoming and warm. With its huge expanses of mountains, rainforests and coastlines, Colombia is physically one of the most beautiful countries in the world. It is also a country of both great wealth and deep poverty that has a long history of civil war and violence, in recent decades much of it having to do with the drug trade. Sadly, those more sensational traits are the ones that often draw attention to Colombia and are highlighted in the international media. For these reasons, it often seems the most common stereotypes of Colombia are negative.

So people ask us if we felt safe when we traveled there to adopt, or if we "saw anything [illicit]" going on. I've been told my kids "won the jackpot" when they left Colombia and became American citizens. Once, a fellow classmate in a general parenting class, someone I barely knew, asked me if I'd "brought anything else back" when I adopted my son, putting a finger to her nose and sniffing as if snorting cocaine. *Really.*

Before I adopted my children and had the opportunity to experience Colombia for myself, I'm sure I had similar associations with the country—if I thought about it at all. And then, as probably happens to most international travelers, when I actually visited the country, I found Colombia to be quite different from the stereotypes. People go to Sunday dinner with their families in Colombia. People work in cubicled offices in Colombia. Colombian children play at the park while their mothers chat on benches nearby. Colombian grocery stores sell Pop Tarts and fresh fruit. Colombian couples take walks in the evenings and drive into the country on their days off. Much about Colombia ended up being quite familiar to me.

I did not anticipate how protective I would feel of Colombia and its reputation as a result of adopting from there. I have a deep affection for Colombia, and I want other people to value it, as well. I came to find out that part of my responsibility as my children's mother is to highlight the Colombia with which people aren't always familiar. So I am something of an ambassador for Colombia. I have to make an effort to share or explain aspects of Colombia to those without first-hand knowledge of the country. I want my kids to feel good about being from Colombia. I want them to know we are proud of this aspect of them and proud to be a part-Colombian family. If your loved ones adopt internationally, they will probably be proud of the connection to another country their child brings to the family, as well.

Choosing to emphasize a country's positive aspects is not

to say that an adoptive family will ignore or deny that country's very real problems. They can't; these issues are likely fundamental factors in the child's adoption. But the negative realities will probably be discussed in ways that take into primary consideration the child's well-being and the importance of a positive relationship with his country of origin. So that probably means that, for a long time, these discussions about a country's less positive aspects will happen between adults or within the core family.

If your loved ones adopt internationally, the family will be grateful to you if you regard the sending country with respect and positive interest. Show your regard by educating yourself about the child's country of origin—its history, its geography, its people, its place in global affairs. Sometimes extended family members even join the parents on their adoption travels. As a friend or relative, you get to celebrate the best parts of the birth country, reinforcing its value to the child because it is his place of origin. Perhaps the adoptive family—perhaps *your* family—is now or will soon be part-Ethiopian or part-Chinese or part–Korean or part-something-else. Describe them as such—as a German-Vietnamese or Polish-Ecuadorian family. Depending on your relationship with the family, you might let the kids hear you *authentically* praise aspects of their origins. Mention how beautiful you find traditional Indian art or the great Ukrainian restaurant you found. Admire the influential history of China or beautiful features typical of its people. Repeat an interesting news item from the child's birth country.

Take advantage of the opportunity that international adoption affords to make a very personal connection with another part of the world. Demonstrate your willingness to welcome and value the whole child, including the geographical and cultural origins he may bring to the family.

Orphanages and institutions

Another aspect of an adoptive child's personal history has to do with the conditions in which they lived prior to their adoption. Practices for the care of children available for adoption vary around the world. Currently, in the United States, children who are not adopted immediately at birth typically live in foster care until they are adopted, rather than in the large group settings (orphanages) once common. (In fact, "orphanage" is often considered an inaccurate term as many children, though available for adoption, do have living birthparents who have relinquished their parental rights or had them terminated. And some of these institutions also provide care for children whose parents have no intention of relinquishing their parental rights but are financially or physically unable to parent them.) Most children adopted internationally have lived either in a foster home or within a larger organization: an institution.

To some, the words *orphanage* and *institution* may evoke images of unclean, crowded living spaces filled with abandoned, underdeveloped children receiving insufficient care and little attention, of too many children among too few caregivers. These negative associations are the result of some very real and very tragic situations that have existed around the world and throughout history—and continue to exist to this day. But it's important to know that though these conditions do exist at some institutions for children, there are also many, many fine organizations providing attentive care for children, often in difficult circumstances, as well.

In recent years, government-level attention has been paid to standards and practices of adoption and care for children awaiting adoption worldwide. One major international agreement, the Hague Convention on Adoption, attempts to impose safeguards on adoption intended to ensure that adoptions between countries are legal and ethical and that the interests of the children are paramount. One byproduct of these safeguards should be heightened attention to standards for the care and conditions of adoptable children. In the United States, adoptive parents are strongly encouraged to adopt from countries which have met and signed the strict requirements of the Hague Convention on Adoption, both to ensure the legitimacy of their own adoption and to further support enhanced standards for adoption and care of children.

Though it's never ideal that a child live in a non-family environment, it's a reality for children around the world, including, of course, the United States. It's understandable—even important—to have fear and anxiety about the global conditions in which children are living, especially the child or children adopted by your loved ones. Having these reservations means you're aware of disparities domestically and around the world. But most of us are familiar with some version of an *Adoption Horror Story* having to do with children from foster care or institutions. So, in the spirit of telling *Adoption Success Stories* instead, I'd like to offer the story of one family's orphanage experience: my own.

Our foundation

We brought our two oldest children with us when we traveled to adopt our third child because we wanted them to be there to welcome their new sister into our family. We also wanted them to visit their birth country. It was important to us that they have an opportunity to experience again the people and culture from which they came. One part of our trip involved a visit to the "foundation" (the organization prefers this word to "orphanage" or "institution") in which the children spent the earliest period of their lives, before we adopted them.

Our youngest daughter had been presented to us at the home of the foundation's director, so we'd had her for a few days before we had the opportunity to return to the building itself. As we pulled into the parking lot, we noticed nurses, their arms holding young children, looking out at us from a second-floor window. My husband and I waved and they waved back. Then we took the two oldest children from the car and the second-floor waving became more enthusiastic as the nurses recognized that we must be a family returning with children who'd once lived there. We finally took out our youngest, who had left their care just days before, and displayed her for the windows above. At this point, the nurses even waved the little arms of the babies they held.

When we entered the building, we were greeted by staff and nurses, all eager to see the youngest child, she who was still *their* child, as well. She was lifted from my arms and passed from nurse to nurse, fingers touching her new dress, voices admiring her baggy little tights. The words they used! She was their *princesa*, their *muñeca* or "little doll," even *mi vida*, "life" itself. People looked out of their offices at the sound of our happy noise and hurried over when they saw who was causing it.

As a family, we were led through the building, viewing the crib in which our child had slept, where she'd had her baths and had her food prepared. Everywhere, voices lifted, faces turned to see the child and her new family.

I began to introduce my two older children. "Ah!" The nurses called to each other and those who had cared for my older children turned their eyes and their embraces on them as well. I could see it was real. They truly remembered them.

I have seen the rocking chairs in which my children were held and the colorful rooms that stimulated their young senses. I have heard the sounds of the women's voices and the soft music that accompanied their days at the foundation. Orphanages, no matter how well-run or well-staffed, are never a substitute for parents. But organizations like this one exist around the world, staffed by devoted people doing their best in difficult conditions to care for their young residents, some of whom may one day be adopted. And many even extend support services to the biological families—offering things like parenting classes for birthparents who have other children, further education, or job skills training to improve their prospects for the future.

Of course, these are not the situations in which all children awaiting adoption start their lives. Some children live with their birth or extended families for months or even years before placement. Some live in foster homes.

And the hard truth is that the early environments of adoptive children are not always pleasant, and not always easy to think about. No doubt, some begin their lives in situations in which they did not receive even nearly adequate care and may even have been seriously damaged by their experience. But it's important to try to value the efforts and intentions of the child's caregivers, regardless of the environment in which the child may have resided. Many children form deep bonds with them and with other children around them. My family views with affection and deep gratitude the early caretakers of my children. Other adoptive families do, too.

Welcoming the whole child

Positive or negative, consciously or not, adoptive children bring their history—people, places and experiences—with them to their families. This is true for any adoption, domestic or international, infant or older child. For friends and relatives around the adoptive family, it may seem preferable to love only the child who has arrived, trying to forget or ignore the early history that arrives with her. It makes sense to want the child to be totally enfolded into the new family, offering her a fresh start and a new life. But the child's history is important—precious even—to adoptive parents because it is part of what comprises their child.

Within this discussion of valuing a child's background, it is important to clarify that there is a balance that must be struck between acknowledging the value of someone's personal history and compromising their privacy. Thus certain aspects of a child's origins—the facts around the birthmother, the circumstances behind the adoption and the conditions of their early life—are typically ones that only the adoptive parents and, later, the older adoptive child, should broach. Many adoptive parents don't talk much about these parts of a child's adoption, considering it to be the child's information to share, not their own. Even if you're very close to the parents, it's quite possible you may never discuss with them these specific aspects of their child.

You can, in your own attitude toward the child and adoption, have compassion and respect for what the child brings with him, recognizing that these are real and essential parts of the child. But it is crucial that the child's privacy be respected and preserved. Facts of the child's personal history must be judiciously disseminated by the adoptive parents and the adoptive child *only*, if at all. Privacy is a critical issue in adoption and deeply relevant to those around the adoptive family. The following chapter is devoted to this important topic in adoption.

What you can do

Try to consider the birthmother with compassion and respect. Recognize her ongoing role in the family. Value her as part of the child's personal history.

Recognize that aspects of a child's origins accompany him to his family and thus become part of the family.

If a child was adopted internationally, try to respect the policies and procedures of the sending country. Refrain from disparaging systems or cultures that may be unfamiliar or confusing.

Resist negative assumptions about a child's prior living conditions. Recognize that organizations and caregivers worldwide are working on behalf of children awaiting adoption, often in difficult circumstances.

Know that every adoptive child arrives with a personal history. Welcome it as part of the child. Consider whether and how certain aspects of a person's history should ever be known and discussed outside of the adoptive family.

6

The child's right to privacy

When my husband and I were in the process of completing our first adoption, an established adoptive family invited us to their house to talk with us and answer some of our questions about adoption. Feeling all flush with adoption information and maybe wanting to demonstrate just how ready I felt I was to become part of the adoption community, I asked what I thought was an insider's question. I asked, in front of their 6-year-old child, what they knew about his birthmother. Looking back, I see just how gracious his mother was. She glanced at her son, who appeared to be occupied with his cars (though now that I've watched my own son look busy while eavesdropping, I realize that this boy was completely tuned in to our conversation), and said to me, "You know, that's not something we talk about outside of our family." Of course it wasn't. I was breaching the boy's privacy. I could still kick myself for asking that question. I wish I'd known better. But karma being what it is, I've now had plenty of opportunities to try to respond graciously to other people's personal questions about my children.

People sometimes ask adoptive parents questions of a far more intimate nature than they'd ask a biological parent. From an adoptive parents' point of view, "What do you know about the birthmother?" is a question just as presumptuous as asking a biological parent "What method did you use to get pregnant?" People who were adopted do not forgo their right to the same level of privacy as others. An adoptive child has no less a right to privacy about his personal information than any grown-up or non-adoptive child.

That said, there is valid confusion about what is private adoption information and what is okay to ask about. The not-very-satisfying answer is that boundaries around privacy are likely different for every family and will differ from person to person.

Adoptive parents struggle with the public/private nature of adoption all the time. They are challenged to balance their family's sometimes obvious public status as an adoptive family with the privacy of the family's individuals. Most adoptive families are proud of their families and want to present a positive attitude about adoption to others, particularly their children. The precarious task for adoptive parents is to be open enough about adoption that their children don't see adoption as a secret or as something to be ashamed of, while at the same time taking care not to compromise the right to privacy of everyone involved. So, even as they're trying to protect their children's privacy, adoptive parents are also trying to normalize adoption for their children and for others around them.

An important reason that parents try to control the dissemination of their child's information has to do with the fact that the child himself—particularly a young child—often does not yet know all of his own personal information. Parents are responsible for safeguarding facts about the child's life for the child until he or she is of an appropriate age to hear it. If the child's information becomes too commonly known, adoptive parents risk the child hearing things before he or she is ready. One adoptive mother tells of her daughter learning she had biological siblings in a very abrupt way, when another sibling used it to wound her in an argument. The parent had intended to discuss this under gentler circumstances, and when she felt her daughter was ready to hear it. This mother wished she'd been more careful about sharing her daughter's personal information with others, even within her own family.

Privacy Plans

Until the child is old enough to manage his own personal information, it is your loved ones' very important responsibility to maintain and protect the child's privacy on his behalf. Adoptive parents need to actively think through what information is "in-house," and what information is for public consumption. One family kept two photo albums of their new son. One, the "public" album, remained on the coffee table for viewing by all of the visitors coming to see their child. It documented bath times and park visits and other images typical of any new family. Another "private" album was for just the immediate family and included things like pictures of the child's foster family, the first meeting between the parents and child, and other very personal moments in the inception of this new family.

I suggest that new adoptive parents—including those still in the adoption process—develop for themselves what I call a Privacy Plan. They decide what information is off-limits (e.g., birthparent information, certain details about early living conditions, specific reasons the child was available for adoption) and have a plan for responding to inappropriate questions. For example, when someone asks me what I "know about" my child's birthmother or for some other information about his personal history, I've developed a standard reply: "That's not my information to share." I try to keep it simple; I say it lightly and move on. People usually get the idea pretty quickly. They don't mean to overstep. Often they've just never thought of it that way before.

Some parents will be comfortable sharing some of the intimate information about their children with those close to them—some may, in fact, share more than you might want to know about a child's personal history. Not every adoptive parent has developed boundaries around their child's privacy nor has it occurred to them to do so. But I've long been guided by the experience of one adult adoptee who recalled how much it bothered her to hear her mother talk about her adoption with strangers who approached them when they were out in public (grocery stores again). She felt that her private life was being discussed casually with people she didn't even know. But until she was old enough to articulate her own feelings, her mother was unaware that she was compromising her daughter's privacy.

Sometimes an adoptive family will encounter someone who really presses them for information, who feels they have the right to know all about a child's personal history, often because the child is now a relative. Know that, in general, unless it's a health issue or some other aspect of background that impacts how you interact with the child *at present*, you are probably not entitled to detailed information about the child's background before the time that the child entered the family. Much of a child's personal information can wait until such time as the child can choose to share it himself.

So where is the middle ground? The fact of an adoption is not something to be ignored or treated as a secret. And you will have questions. Following are a few rules of thumb to follow when it comes to asking questions about a child and his adoption:

Not in front of the child

Critically, no matter what adoption questions you have, try not to ask them in front of the child. It's a recurring complaint among adoptive parents that people ask inappropriate questions in front of their children (as in me asking about the birthmother in front of the child). Even if you feel assured that any question you have is legitimate, the parents will thank you for asking it out of the child's presence. Remember that even a child's adoptive status is not a matter for casual conversation (i.e., "Was he adopted?"). In fact, many adoptive parents—though they may make significant eye contact or vague comments indicating a mutual recognition when they encounter other apparently adoptive families—say they try to respect the privacy of their children and other adoptive children and don't comment on or question their apparent connection with strangers.

Ask yourself: why do I want to know?

There's an important new person in the life of your loved ones and you want to know everything about them. But before you ask a question about the child, in order to determine whether it may be relevant, one strategy is to ask yourself, "Why do I want to know this?" If you don't have a good answer, maybe it's not information you need to have. Ask yourself if you *should* know about things like the existence of siblings or the role of a birthfather before the child is able to know and understand it himself. Remember that *it's the child's information first*, even if he doesn't yet know all of it.

Don't take boundaries personally

Do try not to take it personally if you're told, hopefully graciously, that certain information is off-limits to you. You don't mean to intrude. But parents have to let you know where their boundaries stand—it's part of their responsibility to the child. If you have questions, consider framing them so that they show you recognize there are boundaries around some information: "Please let me know if I'm overstepping, but I wondered . . ."

All of the child's information is precious

Finally, it's helpful if those who hold any private information about the child are careful not to treat it casually. It's not fodder for small talk; rather it's precious and should be treated as such. Sometimes you will have the opportunity to discuss the child's adoption with someone who doesn't know the family or the child. Remember that you show respect for the child and for adoption by preserving the child's privacy, even when you don't have to.

When it comes to protecting a child's privacy, you can provide tremendous support to your loved ones: by understanding what information is personal, by respecting the family's boundaries, and by protecting information on behalf of the child. The next chapters offer further suggestions for talking about adoption. And they discuss how it's likely you, as a friend or relative, will at times be called upon to represent and protect the interests of the child and their adoption.

What you can do

Understand the child's right to own his own personal history, some of which he may not even yet know himself.

Differentiate between secrets and privacy. Adoption is not a secret. But some information about an adoption will remain private. Recognize what information is and is not necessary for you to know about a child's background.

Understand the parents' responsibility to protect their child's privacy until such time as the child can do so for himself. Don't take it personally when they enforce boundaries around information.

Refrain from asking about the child's personal history in front of the child.

Demonstrate respect for the practice of adoption by maintaining the privacy of others—even when you don't have to. Avoid sharing the family's personal information, even with people who don't know the family.

7

Talking about adoption

If you want to see some fireworks, get a group of adoptive parents together and ask them, "What's the strangest thing anyone has ever said to you about adoption?" All adoptive parents can probably provide a list of "The Things People Have Said" to them about their kids and about adoption. A few highlights from my own list include:

Did you think about adopting from Utah? There are lots of white babies there and people don't drink.

If it's a boy, you're thinking about naming him Peter? Don't you mean Pedro?

Aren't you afraid of not attaching?

How much did he cost?

Does she [an infant] speak Spanish?

I always thought adopted kids were weird.

White people only adopt children of other races because they can't get a white baby.

Wow. I just don't think I could ever adopt. (Right. In front. Of my kids.)

At the time they were made, many of these comments stung. With some time and perspective, I now realize most of them simply reflect a lack of knowledge or familiarity with adoption. But it didn't feel good to hear them. And I do remember them.

But, really, how are others to know what's okay to say and what might offend or alienate an adoptive parent? Questions that may seem benign to the person asking them can come across as too personal or even disrespectful to the adoptive parents or the child. Comments meant to show you have a general familiarity with adoption can end up provoking new or prospective parents. You may worry you'll inadvertently say the wrong thing or ask the wrong question (and "wrong" can be very subjective). But if you don't say anything, the adoptive parents might assume that you don't support the adoption. That can happen, too.

Ideally, adoptive parents take responsibility for gently educating or correcting those who inadvertently misstep. But that may mean addressing a lot of people. And when adoptive parents are immersed in the newness and stress of the adoption process (to be followed by the general upheaval of life as a parent), they may find they're just more willing to be annoyed than they are to perform the role of adoption educator—fair or not. I know I was far more sensitive to the words of others when I was still getting comfortable with adoption myself. And like anyone else, adoptive parents don't always know quite where their boundaries lie around this new aspect of their lives—not until the first unfortunate person steps over them (at which point they become quite clear). So while adoptive parents have some responsibility for explaining and guiding, they're not always able to do so.

There are a few common adoption-related questions and comments that most adoptive parents hear a lot and would prefer not to—and they're things that others can easily avoid. Some of them are inappropriate because they infringe on the child's and family's privacy. Others have to do with showing basic respect to the privilege that is adoption. You may find you have said some of these things. I've certainly said some of these things. And I bet the adoptive parents for whom you're reading this book have said some of these things, as well. For most of us, knowing how to talk respectfully about adoption required some education and experience. And still we make mistakes.

The suggestions that follow are intended to provide explanation and to offer some guidelines. They are absolutely *not* intended to silence friends and relatives who want to discuss adoption with the family. Adoptive parents will likely value most that you show you are interested in their adoption and in their child by talking with them, even if it involves some awkward moments. One adoptive mother notes sadly that her mother has never once asked her anything about her adoption—the adoption of her own granddaughter, now a grade-schooler. The grandmother might have been opposed to the adoption or afraid of offending her daughter, but saying nothing, asking no questions, provided no opportunity for either of them to address any possible reservations and concerns. Her mother's silence was deeply hurtful to the adoptive mother. She would have preferred her mother ask even potentially offensive questions so that she'd at least have the chance to educate her mother and try to allay her fears. So most important, *talk*.

I look at it this way: talking about adoption is a little like trying to speak the local language in another country. You might make some mistakes, but people usually appreciate the effort.

One to avoid

Many, many adoptive parents with whom I've talked about adoption—especially those who first considered adoption following infertility—cited this first comment as *the worst thing people said* when they told others they were adopting. These parents advise that no matter how much personal or anecdotal evidence you have, no matter how well-intentioned you are or how much you think it's what the parents want to hear, please *don't tell someone that as soon as they adopt, they will get pregnant*. Full disclosure: I've done this myself. (In fact, according to research by RESOLVE: The National Infertility Association, only about 5% of women become pregnant after adopting, the same percentage of women who have infertility and who do not adopt.)

Remember: adoption is not a strategy for attaining a

biological child. When someone announces that they're adopting, they're announcing the coming arrival of their child, their *adoptive* child. For adoptive parents, a biological child is not the focus for them by this point, if indeed it ever was. In fact, even before they meet their child, the adoptive parents often already love the child, and have begun their relationship with the child. Others may mean it as a positive thing, but please understand that to promote a pregnancy now is dismissive, if not downright disrespectful, of the coming adoptive child, as well as of the great effort and consideration that went into the adoption decision.

Real-natural-biological-birth

Another common mistake people make is to refer to the biological or birth parent as the "real" parent. Someone might ask something like "Where is his real mother?" They know who they're referring to. And the adoptive parents know who they're referring to. But the gentlest response a person will get from an adoptive parent will be something along the lines of "I'm right here." So, quite simply, the adoptive parent is always the "real" parent. Along the same lines, she is also the "natural" one. It's best to avoid calling anyone else the "real mother" or "natural father."

If you were to talk about the woman who gave birth to and then relinquished the child, it's appropriate to refer to her as the "birthmother" or "biological mother" (remembering that it's always important to consider the child's right to privacy before discussing birth families). Some adoptive children refer to their biological mother as their "first mother." Some people, particularly in an open adoption, will refer to the birthmother by her first name. I'd suggest you follow the parents' lead on that one.

By extension, it's not appropriate to ask about a child's "real" siblings. I have three children, biologically unrelated (a fact I cite here only because it is relevant to this discussion and to this audience of readers). They are "really" each other's brother and sisters. Imagine for a moment what it sounds like to them to hear people ask if they are "real brother and sister." Trust me, the bickering and the clobbering are the product of very "real" and very "natural" sibling relationships. If they weren't real siblings they'd have to treat each other better.

Along these lines, sometimes people ask about my children "Do they have the same mother?" They sure do; she's standing right in front of you looking peevish. Whether the kids share a biological connection is not a topic for casual conversation. One adoptive parent calls it "inside information," and thus not usually necessary for those outside the immediate family.

These are common words and terms that other people will sometimes use with you and with others. They may be irksome but they're likely not ill-intended. By using appropriate adoption language yourself, you can help to change others' perceptions of what makes "real" families and "real" parents or relatives. (And it's a way to show that you're in on it, too.)

"Lucky"

Some people use the word "luck," others refer to "blessings." Either, both—there's plenty of it in adoption. But *how* the words "lucky" and "blessed" are used to talk about adoption deserves a little attention.

Before the adoptive child arrives, you are probably rooting for the adoptive parents, maybe saying things like: "You're going to be great parents. Any child will be lucky to get you." You love and support the parents and know that anyone who gets to be their child will indeed be lucky—and/or blessed—to have them. That's one way that you show them that you, too, want them to become parents.

And by calling the child "lucky," you may also be recognizing that adoption provides a child a chance at a safer, healthier life than she might otherwise have. It's possible that were the child to remain in her original circumstances she would grow up in severe poverty or in unsafe conditions. Perhaps without adoption, she would never have access to a basic education or become a part of a permanent family. These are very real issues and, obviously, some of the primary impetus for adoptions worldwide. And not every child available for adoption finds a place in an adoptive family. It is generally a good thing for a child awaiting adoption to be adopted.

However, and I didn't know this until after my first adoption, I've come to learn that adoptive children may be confused and even offended by being told that they are "lucky" that they were adopted. It's like being told they are on the receiving end of someone else's charity. It dismisses their own essential contributions to the family. "They're so lucky" can end up sounding to a child's ears like "you should be grateful." We don't want to put that burden on kids. One of the most remarkable things about adoption is the intense reciprocal nature of it. As in most families, family members are grateful for—and lucky to have—each other. One adoptive mother said this: "Don't put adoptive parents on pedestals for adopting children; it's as good for us as it is for them."

In fact, many adoptive parents consider themselves "the lucky ones." As an adoptive mother, I don't look at my little cherubs refusing to eat their dinner and think, "I am so generous and good. I have given these lucky children a home. And broccoli." No, I say to them, "Eat your broccoli" (while thinking, "I am so lucky to have these children who are refusing to eat their broccoli").

Using words like "adopted" and "adoptive"

In general, to refer to someone's adoption or adoptive status is almost always unnecessary. If you think about it, there is almost never a reason to describe a child along the lines of "their adopted daughter." Do people go around referring to "my biological son" or "my birth children"? It's the same thing, right? Thus, it is also respectful to refer to your loved one's child as "my grandchild" or "my best friend's son," without using "adoptive" as a qualifier. (You would arrive at this conclusion on your own with regard to your loved ones; be sure to extend this courtesy to other people who were adopted, too.)

Throughout this book, I refer to myself as an "adoptive mother." I do that only for clarification and for the purposes of this book. In ordinary life, I rarely call myself an "adoptive" parent and neither will your loved ones. I think of myself only as my children's mother, with no qualifiers at all. I am just their mom. The one with the uneaten broccoli.

You might begin to notice now how this comes up in the media. Reporters and newscasters don't mention it when a newsmaker has been raised by his biological parents. But if the news involves someone who was adopted, the media will often refer to them as "adopted" or otherwise highlight the fact that a person was adopted. I always ask myself, "Why'd they include the fact that she was adopted? How was that relevant to the story?" It almost never is. This kind of usage can perpetuate negative stereotypes about adoption and people who were adopted.

Another suggestion for precise adoption language has to do with the way we use the word "adopted." It's common to hear the word "adopted" used as an adjective to describe someone (e.g., "he *is adopted*"). Some people prefer that adoption be considered an event—something that happened—not a condition. So to have been adopted is just one event—albeit one of the most significant—in a person's life (e.g., "she *was adopted*").

This view is not consistent, even within the adoption community. One adult adoptee explains that she uses the phrase "I am adopted," because, for her, adoption is "a fundamental part of my experience and who I am today."

For me, when it's relevant, I say my children "were adopted," meaning the adoption was an action that took place and was completed. I don't say they "are adopted." My children will make their own informed decisions around these terms, as will your loved ones, and as should you.

But again, while it's correct to use the word "adoptive" or to say someone "was adopted" to describe their status as a person who has had that experience, it's almost always extraneous information. Maybe it's like the quality of being left-handed. You wouldn't refer to someone as "her left-handed daughter." You'd probably only mention their left-handedness when it was relevant, like figuring out seating arrangements. And how often do we talk seating arrangements? That's about how often we need to talk about someone's adoptive status.

Unfortunately, it's also common for the practice of adoption and words like "adopted" to be applied casually or colloquially to situations unrelated to actual adoption. It's important not to treat adoption too lightly, to use it as an insult or as the point of a joke about a person who was not adopted (e.g., "You're the only athlete in the family. You must be adopted." "We told her if she didn't stop fighting with her sister we'd put her up for adoption"). Some people object to things like highways and pets being "adopted." Those touched by adoption (including you) will appreciate when others treat the concept of adoption with care, using the language of adoption with seriousness and respect.

Stereotypes limit our ability to know each other

I once watched a woman observe a boy's poor playground behavior (the boy was not her son) and murmur to her friend, "He was adopted," as if that was an explanation for the boy's shouting and grabbing of sand toys. I've heard the athletic skills of an adopted child discounted by a parent from an opposing team who said, "Of course he's a great hockey player. He's from Russia!" These kinds of comments and attitudes draw unnecessary attention to the child's adoptive status (compromising their privacy). They also perpetuate stereotypes.

You don't want to know a stereotype; you want to know a person. As part of your own adoption education, consider examining your stereotypes. We all have them. What might you expect of this child (even unconsciously), based on their background, their personal history or ethnicity? What are your expectations of someone who was adopted? Acknowledging your stereotypes is the first step in overcoming them. This is important to do because, positive or negative, stereotypes are limiting. They keep us from fully knowing a person.

Remember that, using the Russian-born hockey player as example, a child is not a good hockey player *because* he's from Russia (a stereotype). Instead, he is like lots of other talented athletes, some of whom are also Russian, all of whom have had to work hard to be successful, just like him. And a child should be able to have a temper tantrum on the playground or get in trouble at school without their less-than-ideal behavior being attributed to an adoption stereotype. It's not fair to the child and it's not fair to you. Try not to allow stereotypes or expectations limit your relationship with the child.

Do talk

Race, family, personal histories—these are tricky subjects, regardless of whether they're related to adoption. And everyone's experiences with and boundaries around these topics are different. Some parents are offended by questions that others find innocuous. A comment made by a family member may be interpreted differently than the same comment from a stranger.

The topic of adoption is approached differently by every adoptive family and by every individual therein. But, though guidelines are important, most important is that you do talk with the parents about their child and about adoption. Don't play it too safe and try to ignore their experience. Remember, like any parent, the adoptive parents know that their children are the smartest, funniest, and most beautiful in the world, and they will relish any opportunity to explain this to you.

(A list of suggested *Conversation starters* on the topic of adoption can be found at the end of the book.)

Nice things to hear

Adoptive parents suggest the following as some of their favorite things that people said to them about their adoptions:

Congratulations!

How are you feeling about things?

I'm so happy for you. You're going to be great parents.

How can I help?

Can we throw you a shower?

Do whatever you think is best. I just want you to be happy.

Is there anything about his background that you want us to know?

You have a beautiful family.

I'd love to hear your adoption story.

You are all so lucky to have each other.

8

People will ask you *questions: Representing the child and adoption*

Hᵒʷ'ᵈ *she get so brown?"* My mother's neighbor startled her with this question one morning as she was out walking with my daughter. Later, after telling me about the incident, she remarked that when my husband and I adopted, she'd figured *we'd* get plenty of questions about the children and about adoption, but she hadn't expected to be answering those types of questions herself. Nor had it occurred to me that other people close to my children might also find themselves responding to questions and comments about the children and about adoption. My mother didn't feel prepared to answer her neighbor as effectively as she'd have liked (and this is a lady who likes to be able to answer someone—effectively).

When your loved ones decided to adopt, it may have seemed that your primary role would be that of an observer or cheerleader, and eventually that of a friend or relative to the family. Like my mother and me, you may not have realized that people might ask *you* questions about adoption and the child. People may make remarks to you about the child or about adoption that make you uncomfortable and that you'll want to address or correct. And there may be times that you feel you need to protect someone's privacy or integrity, particularly that of the child. You'd probably like to feel at least a *little* prepared.

The suggestions that follow provide some ideas for replying to some of the potential questions and comments you might get about adoption and the child. You've probably found you had some misconceptions about adoption yourself. You will have become much more knowledgeable about adoption just by observing the process and experience of your loved ones. But know that you needn't worry if you fumble a response or later find yourself thinking, "What I should have said is . . ." I've found that someone else always comes along to provide another opportunity to try out a better answer.

Most important: you are speaking for the child

No matter who asks the question, or how uncomfortable the circumstances, when you're called upon to discuss a child and his adoption, it's important to think of the child as your real audience. After all, you are really speaking on the child's behalf. Any response should be that which you'd want the child to hear. Whenever someone asks me questions about my children or adoption, I try to ask myself, "What's the best answer—*for my child?*" and then answer accordingly.

This is especially important to consider because people

may ask you questions about the child and his adoption in front of the child. Even if the child is not yet of an age when he can understand what you're saying, try to speak as if for him. It's good practice. But whether he's physically present or not, always try to frame your answer according to what the child might (or might not) want shared.

Some adoption-related questions you might be asked include:

Is she adopted?
Where's she from?
What [ethnicity] is she?
Why did they adopt?
Couldn't they [her parents] have children of their own?

So, taking the approach that the child is your primary audience, consider your answers with two goals in mind:

To protect the child's privacy and integrity, and his right to a sense of normalcy.

To reinforce the child's adoption and background as positive and permanent things for the child and family.

You might rehearse your replies to these kinds of questions. For example, the question "Is he adopted?" still catches me off guard (in the grocery store and elsewhere). For me, it's an aspect of our family that I'm really proud of, but it's also a pretty intimate aspect of us, and it always feels abrupt coming from a stranger. I don't want to share private information, but neither do I want my children to feel it's something of which to be embarrassed.

I've found a few ways to respond. When I do answer, I leave it at a breezy "Yes," and then move us on to another topic (or to another aisle in that grocery store). I've been known to fake that I didn't hear a question, instead smiling pleasantly. To respond to those awkward "What is she?" and "Where is she from?" questions, again, think about what the child needs to hear you say. It's often best to simply keep it simple and give answers like, "She's my niece" or "She's from Sacramento," rather than share their background with a stranger. It may not be the information the questioner sought, but the child hears true and accurate answers to those questions.

Take advantage of your position as a friend or relative, someone in a peripheral position to the child and the adoption. You can always redirect the questioner to the parents: "You'd have to ask her parents that question." You might say something like, "Thanks for asking, but I'm not comfortable answering that question." Or use my own favorite—and quite versatile—answer to questions about my children's backgrounds: "That's not my information to share." It doesn't hurt anyone's feelings and it makes what I hope is a gentle point about the child's right to private information. And one more thing to consider: just because someone asks you a question does not mean you have to answer it. Someone pointed out this wonderful truth to me in my early years as an adoptive mother and was it ever liberating.

Speaking on behalf of the parents and on behalf of adoption

Besides speaking on the child's behalf, there may be times you are asked about the adoptive parents and their adoption choices. Others might ask you questions like:

Why did they adopt?

Why did they adopt from India? (Russia? Ecuador?)

Why didn't they adopt a baby? An older child? A child of their race? A child of another race? In the United States? Internationally?

In answering questions like these, you're not only speaking for the parents, but also on behalf of the practice of *adoption* itself. If someone doesn't know much about adoption, it is sometimes easy for them to judge or criticize others' adoption decisions. But *you* know that people make their adoption choices following deep, deliberate consideration. *You* know that they adopt according to so many things: their abilities—financial, personal, etc.; the options available to them; personal and global circumstances at the time of the adoption; and many other very personal interests, concerns or values. You can tell people this.

If you know specific (but not private) answers and feel confident in your ability to represent the family, you should. Part of making adoption familiar means talking about it openly, with accuracy and respect.

Ask the adoptive parents themselves for suggestions about how they'd like you to talk about adoption—and theirs in particular—when other people ask you about it. This provides an opportunity for them to explain their preferences as well as their boundaries. They might have very specific messages and observations they'd like to share. For some parents, there's a religious or faith-based aspect to adoption that they want to emphasize: "God brought us together." For others, there are sociological messages they'd like to impart "Children around the world don't live like we do here." If it allies with your own beliefs about adoption, you might decide to mirror their approach.

Talking to non-adoptive children about adoption

Sometimes, friends and relatives of adoptive families discover they need to explain the practice of adoption to children, often their own children. Maybe you are a parent with a child asking how a new baby arrived without the mother ever being pregnant. Perhaps your child's newest cousin was adopted or she's wondering why a certain girl in her classroom looks so different from her parents. A child may want to know why her friend's new brother arrived at age five and speaking a different language. These are good questions!

One way to describe adoption to young children is by explaining that "Not all babies grow in the belly of the mommy that they live with" (though they do all come from a woman). Adoption also presents opportunities to talk with children about disparities and differences in the world and to discuss why there are children in the United States and across the globe in need of families. Of course, whatever you tell a child should be age-appropriate. An early explanation might be something like "Sometimes a woman can't take care of her baby so she finds a family to take care of him." My own son used to explain that he was not born from me because I'm "allergic" to babies in my belly. Until he was old enough to understand the biology behind conception, that early understanding worked fine.

Adoption can be a confusing—even scary—concept to children, whether they were adopted or not. To dispel the fear and confusion, there are two main messages all kids need to hear when it comes to understanding adoption. First is that all families—especially their own—are permanent. *Forever* is a good word to use with kids when talking about families (e.g., "Our family is forever"). Second, kids should understand that there are many ways to create a family, each just as valid and authentic as the others. One adoptive parent explains to children that there are both "born-into" families, and families that are created by adoption.

Children seek security and order, so they might ask questions like these:

Why didn't his [biological] mom keep him?
Is he sad?
Is his mommy sad?
Can someone else adopt him?
Was I adopted?
Would you give me up for adoption? Could I be adopted?

My own young nephew's initial, immediate reaction to my family's first adoption was fear and confusion. He thought he *knew* that all babies are born by their mothers (the ones that are raising them). Adoption threatened his early sense of the way things should be. He was relieved that he had come straight from his own mom's belly. And when he first began to understand that I had adopted my child—his cousin—and what that meant, he had trouble understanding why I was okay with it.

My nephew is one of the most inherently empathetic people I've ever met, and I think he was a little sad for me. He asked me whether I wished that the child—his first adoptive cousin—had come from my belly instead of someone else's. I told him no, I didn't wish that, because my body couldn't produce this child and this child, his cousin, was the child I wanted. I was attentive but firm and spoke to him with confidence about the rightness of things. I felt it was my job—both as his aunt and as my child's mother—to reassure him that all was well, just the way he, as a child, needed it to be.

Since that first adoption, my kind nephew has seen several more cousins come along, including two more who were adopted, and the fear is long gone. Adoption is now just another way that cousins join his family. Some of his cousins come from a pregnant aunt, some he meets for the first time at the airport. They all let him boss them around at Thanksgiving, thus proving the authenticity of the family bond, no matter how they joined it.

Discussing adoption with the child who was adopted

Over time, as you develop a relationship with the child who was adopted, she herself may ask you adoption questions— ones about adoption in general or about her own particular story. You can help to reassure a child that adoption is normal and that her family is right, *real*, and permanent. Consider telling her about what a privilege her adoption is, how much and how eagerly she was awaited, how hard her parents worked to adopt her, and what an important part of the family she is. Notice the *genuine* ways in which the child is like her parents or her family. And of course you don't have to wait for the child to bring up the subject to talk to her about her family. They're nice things to share independent of the big topic of "Adoption."

It's actually not unusual for a child to discuss their adoption and their adoption-related feelings with people other than their parents. In fact, it's common for older children to worry about hurting their parents by asking them questions about their adoption or by sharing feelings about adoption that are not wholly positive. To the child, you may at times feel like a safer person to whom to ask those questions and express those emotions. A child may share with you that he feels sad or angry about things like being different from many of those around him or about missing aspects of his personal history. The child should be allowed to feel all of their emotions around adoption and to have them affirmed. Try to listen without negating or trying to correct their feelings (such as telling a child that their adoption made everyone happy, when their experience of adoption includes a more complicated mix of emotions).

Finally, if the child asks you a question for which you don't know the answer, don't know *how* to answer, or don't know whether it's information that the parents have yet shared with the child, err on the side of caution. If you're not sure, suggest to the child that they ask their parents any specific questions related to their background and adoption. Then be sure to follow up with the parents so that they know what questions the child might be having but not asking his parents. It is helpful for adoptive parents to have some insight into how their child is processing their adoption, especially outside the framework of the immediate family. You might remind the parents that you don't want to compromise your relationship with the child—that you want to remain a safe place for the child to talk so that they can take steps to preserve that option for their child. But knowing about what specific adoption issues are on the minds of their children allows adoptive parents to offer them support and resources, and to reinforce for the child that she can safely talk to her parents about adoption, as well.

Making adoption normal
Again, it's important to try to explain and normalize the concept of adoption with others, but particularly with children, both those who were adopted and those who were not. It was with trepidation that I watched my son go off to

kindergarten and realized that he was going to start receiving direct questions and comments about adoption from other kids, some without any prior experience with adoption. I was not always going to be able to influence the messages he got about adoption, ensuring that they were largely positive and affirming. Indeed, it's often from interactions with other children that adoptive kids first get the idea that adoption is unusual or distinctive. One mother told me how her daughter's friend, having learned that the daughter was adopted, reacted by saying, "Oh, no." Another family learned a lesson the summer one cousin told another, "I love you, even though you're not my real cousin." The adults had not done a sufficient job of normalizing adoption as "just another" means of creating family—*real* family. So it's helpful if other, non-adoptive children have a real—and positive—understanding of adoption.

This is an area in which friends and relatives can provide active support for the adoptive family. Help to make adoption normal. Anticipate and celebrate the arrival of an adoptive child just as you would a biological child. If you're a parent, use media depictions—movie and commercials—and the example of other families to gently and proactively illustrate for your child how all families don't look alike or begin in the same way. Children's books are an especially good tool for providing both adults and children with the words for talking about adoption. Show them a child's birth state or country on a map. Give your child the vocabulary to discuss adoption and use appropriate adoption language (e.g., *birthmother* vs. *real* mother). When you talk about where babies come from or how families are made, include adoption. My own daughter—adoptive child that she is—recently said she was going to "have a baby in her belly" and be a mom some day. I responded, "Sure. And maybe you'll adopt a baby, too." And when she paused in her play, as if that had never occurred to her, I realized that I myself need to do a better job of reinforcing adoption as just another path to parenthood.

Become an adoption advocate

Besides answering questions, you may find yourself addressing other people's misconceptions about adoption. You may hear people say inappropriate or inaccurate things about adoption and be in a position to correct them. You may find yourself taking on the role of adoption advocate. One adoptive grandmother takes it as her personal mission to dispel any notion that adoption is simply a matter of placing plump infants into the arms of young, available couples. She makes sure that anyone who speaks casually about adoption knows how hard her daughter worked to adopt and how complicated it had been—and that it had been worth it. One adoptive grandfather writes a letter to the editor every time he sees someone's adoptive status included in an article when he perceives it as irrelevant to the point of the story. You can patronize companies that feature adoptive families in their advertising or that support adoption-related organizations in their community service efforts, sponsorships, and charitable contributions (and let the companies know why you chose them). I wasn't planning a visit to Nebraska, but when their tourism department aired a television commercial featuring an adoptive family, I called the 800 number listed and requested a brochure. Gently correct people's inaccurate language around adoption. Discuss with others what you've learned, the things that surprised you, and the ways in which you've been impacted by adoption.

Over time, most friends and relatives of adoptive families will likely encounter opportunities to speak on behalf of their loved one's adoption, on behalf of the adoptive child, and for the practice of adoption itself. These actions—your advocacy—support adoption and your loved ones and ultimately work to provide a stronger, more informed community around the adoptive family.

What you can do

Expect to be asked questions about the child and about adoption.

Prepare to respond on behalf of the most important audience: the child and the family. Take a positive stance. Maintain privacy.

Ask the parents how they'd like you to respond to anticipated questions and comments.

Help children understand and become comfortable with adoption. Assure them of its rightness. Assure non-adoptive children of their own security and permanence, as well as that of adoptive children.

Know that the adoptive child may one day want to discuss her adoption and the general practice of adoption with you. Provide a safe place to do so. Keep parents informed.

Become an adoption advocate. Normalize and support adoption, both your loved ones' and those of others. Gently correct the erroneous comments or inaccurate adoption language of others.

9

Both an adoptive family and just another *family*

A few years ago, out of the devastating tsunami in the Indian Ocean, came an unusual survival story. A young hippo, later named Owen, lost his hippo family to the huge waves that followed the underwater earthquake. After being rescued by humans, Owen was brought to an animal refuge in Kenya. There he surprised observers by turning to the resident 130-year-old tortoise, Mzee, for comfort and attention—for parenting, some said. A mutual affection developed, and people around the world got the opportunity to view this curiosity via photos of the dusty, deeply-wrinkled tortoise being snuggled by a shiny young hippo. It was a rare feel-good story resulting from this very sad event.

Years later, listening to a talk by a very thoughtful and experienced adoption educator, I heard this story retold from a new angle. This time, it was framed for the audience of adoptive parents as an adoption story, and we were encouraged to share it with our children as such. I should have been pleased. Adoptive parents are always looking for adoption stories to share with their kids. We drop little adoption factoids into casual conversation ("Steven Spielberg adopted some of his kids." "Alexander the Great was adopted. So was Steve Jobs. And Faith Hill. And Luke Skywalker!") So why did this story make my adoptive-parent-hackles rise?

I actually like the tale of Owen and Mzee. I have even read a version of the story to my kids. It's a sweet story with a happy ending. It has a nice message: creatures unrelated to each other can have affection for and take care of one another. And, in general, I think adoption stories that feature animals can offer a safe and comfortable early explanation of adoption for young children. But the story of Owen and Mzee did not initially resonate with me and my experience with adoption at all.

Consider the details of this story. Members of a birth family are swept out to sea, to their deaths. A tortoise (one species) cares for a hippo (another species). To me, that's a pet, not a son. Their pairing is so out-of-the-ordinary that people take pictures and write news articles about it. These are the features of an adoption story?

I certainly didn't identify with the tortoise-as-parent. My children's adoptions were very intentional: like most adoptive children, mine were long- and eagerly-awaited and their arrivals followed years of preparation. They did not join our family in a way that was at all accidental. So what about the hippo's perspective? Will my kids identify with him? Like all adoptive children, mine have experienced loss as a part of their adoptions, but not the violent and dangerous experience of Owen (and certainly of some adoptive children). Nor did they wander in search of a parent; rather, loving, conscientious professionals cared for them and then brought us together.

I had the opportunity to discuss my reaction to this story with the educator who'd suggested it. I explained my resistance to this story being equated with adoption. She is herself an adoptee and invited me to consider the story from a perspective other than as an adoptive parent. First, importantly, she reminded me that she was recommending to parents a very specific version of the story, a children's book that includes a final image of the mother hippo—or Owen's birthmother—watching over him and Mzee. She explained that she's found that the adoptive children with whom she works tend to respond very positively to the idea of a birthmother who is present in Owen's life, even if not as a physical presence. Okay, I could understand that. And where I had resisted the idea of a cataclysmic impetus for adoption as depicted by the tsunami and the death of the mother hippo, she made the point that the tsunami can illustrate the fact that "adoption always happens from something unexpected." It was a useful conversation, adoptee to adoptive parent, and it seemed we both appreciated the story in a new way. And there's room for both viewpoints; they're both valid.

I came to realize that a big reason this story made me uncomfortable is that most adoptive families don't see themselves—nor do they want to be seen—as remarkable. Not in the way that a tortoise parenting a hippo is remarkable. In general, they want to be recognized as just another family, created in a way no more or less valid—or newsworthy—than any other. I wanted the story of Owen and Mzee—if it were to be a story of a family formed through adoption—to be unexceptional.

Thus, after all of the explanations about adoption and adoptive parenting, after all of the requests for special attention to language and specific suggestions for helping adoptive families, after all of the distinctions have been drawn, I'm going to say this about your loved ones, the adoptive family: They are also just another family. Both ordinary and extraordinary.

They go together

I understand that our family pictures have a little more visual variety in them than others. I understand why people's eyes might linger for a moment as they work out the sight of me with my kids. I pretend not to notice when someone does a subtle double-take after my daughter yells, "Watch this, Mom!" in my direction at the park. And I get why people might refer to our family as, "The one with the three kids from Colombia." Though they don't draw the same attention that a tortoise and hippo pairing do, adoptive families, particularly interracial adoptive families, do tend to get noticed.

But adoptive families are on the inside looking out; from that insider's perspective, many consider themselves a well-matched set. That's how they see themselves. For the most part, my children's adoptive status is irrelevant to the way they tease each other or try to avoid eating those vegetables or the way we conduct all of our other business of being a family. Like us, I think most adoptive families appreciate it when others also consider them as just another family.

I understand that for many people adoption is still something of a novelty. When I see a family that looks like my own (parents of one race, kids of another), despite myself, my first thought is usually "adoption." And though it's a reaction based on happy recognition—they're like us!—I would prefer that my own first thought be "family." A family created or expanded through adoption should be unremarkable.

When I discussed this idea—that, ideally, being a family should supersede being an adoptive family—with a friend who has only biological children, she said, "It's like us. We're a family first, and a family with all boys second." She's right. In a way, it's really that simple and universal. Some families are families that camp. Some are families that travel to Mexico every winter. Some do things like fly the Irish flag on St. Patrick's Day and name their kids "Declan" and "Fiona." Some families attend Sunday school, some attend Hebrew school on Saturdays, and others spend their weekends at the beach.

Now I'm certainly not trying to equate *camping* with *adopting*. Within the family, adoption is essential, not extra-curricular. But for those around the adoptive family, those interacting with the family, it usually becomes just another aspect of their family. Yes, adoption is critical to them. It's a wonderful, important, fundamental part of them; but the *adoptive* part is secondary to *family*.

So when *is* it about adoption?

No doubt, the fact of adoption weaves itself into the everyday life of an adoptive family. Besides showing an interest in local politics and community events, the parents may also be conversant in events occurring in another part of the country or the globe. Besides taking karate classes and attending music camp, the child might attend camps or classes that relate to aspects of adoption or of her ethnicity. In our house, the topic of adoption has become a tool for advancing my son's own interests, usually unrelated to adoption. He tries to stay up past his bedtime by announcing in his most serious tones that he'd like to "talk about adoption." I used to drop everything and settle in for a prolonged, soul-searching chat. I've wised up a bit and can now usually gauge his sincerity based on whether he can look me in the eye without giggling.

Typically, there is an ebb and flow to the public role adoption plays in the family. There are indeed moments—even lengthy periods—in which adoptive families do find themselves actively addressing their identity as an adoptive family. In particular, during the adoption process and in the early days with the child, it may seem like the family is all-adoption-all-the-time. And adoptive parents—so preoccupied with the adoption process and then, upon its success, so proud and happy and relieved—often perpetuate that. Then, as the smoke clears and they get used to being a family and begin to immerse themselves in the mundane tasks of everyday parenting, the prevalence of the adoptive aspect of the family is often diminished.

Within the family, the topic of adoption may come up unexpectedly, as when a child is asked about it at school or watches a movie featuring a version of adoption that may evoke questions. At other times, parents might broach the topic of adoption quite intentionally, around a birthday or adoption day, or when reminding kids that they can ask their parents questions about adoption at any time. And as the child ages and confronts the identity issues of any maturing person (though sometimes more complicated for a person who was adopted), it's common that her adoption again plays a more significant role in her life and within the family. These cycles will likely continue. As an adult, it may be the adoptive child who determines whether and to what extent the fact of her adoption becomes a matter for discussion outside the family (though one transracial adoptee reports that even as an adult she still finds herself responding to others' unprovoked questions and comments about her adoptive status).

It's true that adoption is often an additional factor that adoptive parents consider when confronting parenting issues. As one mother put it, "Parents of adopted children are always asking themselves: Is it the age? Or is it adoption?" Another mother described reminding herself, when her 13-year-old's behavior had become increasingly odious, "It's not about adoption; it's about being a teenager." Often it's both. One adult adoptee said, "There's a lot of gray area" when it comes to determining the role that adoption plays in a person's behavior or condition. "It's not always possible to draw a clear line," she said, between whether something is adoption-related or not.

Friends and relatives can take their cues from the parents when it comes to knowing whether to ascribe a child's behavior or emotions to adoption. Sometimes you can help by reassuring the parents ("Every four-year-old acts like that—*you* acted like that!"). And at other times a situation or condition might in fact be directly related to the child's adoption, and you can best help by simply listening without judgment to someone who's having an experience you yourself may not have had. Sometimes it's about adoption, sometimes it isn't. Sometimes adoption is one factor among many. If you are concerned about something—behavior, for example—and wonder if it's adoption-related, a child development book might provide some perspective on what can be expected from a child at a particular age, whether or not they were adopted. But for the most part, whether to define something as adoption-related is for the members of the immediate adoptive family to investigate and decide.

Over time, the fact of the child's adoption will almost certainly become for you just another aspect of the family and of the individual. As my father said once about my children,

"I don't think of them as my 'adoptive grandchildren.'
They're just my grandchildren." This does not negate my
father's deep appreciation for the practice of adoption. And
he acknowledges and respects the ongoing role that adoption
plays in our lives. But he would never categorize any of his
grandchildren as "adoptive" or "biological." My children are
his grandchildren first, without any added qualifiers. If not
immediately, over time, and with some experience behind
you, like most friends and relatives, you will likely arrive at a
similar conclusion about the role that adoption plays in your
relationships with the family and the child.

What you can do

*Understand that "adoptive" is usually secondary in impor-
tance to "family."*

*Let the parents determine the role adoption plays in the pub-
lic life of the family.*

*Let parents determine when and whether to ascribe emotions
or behavior to normal development or to the fact of a child's
adoption.*

*Reinforce for your loved ones that you recognize that, in the
most important ways, they are a family like any other, both
ordinary and extraordinary.*

Conclusion

You're in on it, *too*

I sometimes think of adoption as like being in on a really good secret. Whenever I see a family like ours, I'm always tempted to approach the parents and whisper something like "Can you believe this? Isn't it great?" I suspect that many of them would know exactly what I was talking about. One adoptive parent described to me her reaction to the news that a good friend had unexpectedly become pregnant and stopped the adoption process. She told me, "I was happy for her, of course, but at the same time I felt kind of sad for her because I know what she's missing out on by not adopting." I knew what she meant. But it's an idea that can't really resonate until you're in on it—until you've actually participated in or had the privilege of witnessing a family being expanded by adoption.

You're in on it now, too. You are a member of someone's adoption circle. You are a part of the constellation of adoption. And while there is not, at least as far as I know, a secret handshake, there are experiences and insights to which you are now privy. Like any worthwhile experience, it's likely that adoption will challenge you. And even change you.

I asked friends and relatives of adoptive families to share their thoughts about how they were affected by a loved one's adoption. Some mentioned surprise at their own capacity to change, to accept and enjoy ideas and experiences they hadn't expected. One grandmother said, "It is a blessing to see that you can love [a child who was adopted] just as if they were your biological grandchild." Another relative described an adoption's impact this way: "Now I know that it isn't something to be afraid of. I would tell anyone to consider adoption if they want to have children."

Besides the immediate, emotional benefits of adoption—the relationships that result and the very real joy that children bring—many friends and relatives credit an adoption with having provided them with a heightened global perspective, a broader sense of connection and personal responsibility. One adoptive grandmother credited her grandchildren's adoptions with her "expanded world view." People and communities that may have once felt foreign may begin to seem approachable, and knowable. One relative said about a transracial adoption that it "offered an opportunity to talk about and understand race in a more 'real' way than when it wasn't 'our problem.'" And for some, adoption can clarify or illuminate a connection to humanity. An adoptive uncle described adoption as "a privilege that more people should enjoy and a reminder about the human family."

One of my favorite descriptions of how an adoption affects those around it came from an adult adoptee. He put it this way:

When I think about how we all have grown as a result of adoption in our family, words like open-mindedness, tolerance, understanding, empathy, faith, love, generosity, and selflessness come to mind. Adoption allows us to perceive the world in different ways. It enables us to open our hearts and minds and grow from different and challenging experiences. Adoption challenges our understanding of the traditional family and forces one to go where one may not have considered going on our own.

Finally, in the words of an adoptive grandfather: "Every child gladdens your heart. What happens after a child comes into the family is as important as how they arrived into it." This is where you, the adoptive family's friend or relative, come in. Congratulations. You are in on it now, too.

Conversation starters

Questions to prompt discussion

Following are a few ideas to help friends and relatives begin conversations about adoption with their loved ones.

Questions to ask an adoptive parent:

What aspects of adoption are you most excited about?

What are you looking forward to?

What's the most surprising thing you've learned or experienced in your adoption process?

What worries or fears do you have about adoption?

How do you think parenting through adoption will be like biological parenthood?

How do you think parenting through adoption will be different than biological parenthood?

What joys or benefits do you anticipate adoption will bring to you? Will bring to me?

What challenges do you foresee?

What role do you anticipate the birthmother or birth family will have in your family?

What role do you anticipate the child's birth culture having in the family?

Why were you drawn to adopting this way (i.e., domestically, foster care, international, etc.)? If adopting internationally, why were you drawn to that country?

Do you feel loss or grief around adoption? Can I help you grieve?

Can you describe your boundaries around the child's private information?

People may ask me about your adoption or the child's personal history. How would you like me to answer these kinds of questions?

How can we best prepare for the child that will arrive? Is there anything we should know about prior living conditions that will affect how we interact with him?

When would you like to introduce the child to us?

How can we help with the child's transition into the family? How and when would you like us to be involved?

How can I help you at this stage of your adoption?

How can I help you and your family in the future?

Are there any books, movies, web sites, etc. you'd like me to read or view?

What role would you like me to have in your adoption process and in your life as an adoptive family?

What additional responsibilities do you foresee for me as someone who wants to support an adoptive family?

Is there any other information you'd like me to have at this time?

Questions adoptive parents can ask their friends and relatives:

What do you think of when you think about adoption?

What do you think of when you think of a person who was adopted? Do you have any preconceptions of people who were adopted?

What was adoption like when you were growing up or when you were becoming a parent yourself?

What questions do you have about adoption in general?

What questions do you have about our adoption?

What aspects of adoption are you excited about? What are you looking forward to?

What worries or fears do you have about adoption? About our adoption?

Do you feel loss or grief around adoption? How can I help you grieve?

How much would you like to be involved in our adoption process?

How would you like to be involved in our lives as an adoptive family?

How do you think you might be affected by our adoption?

Is there any other information you'd like to have at this time?

Additional adoption resources for friends and relatives

The books, web sites, articles and organizations listed here provide other perspectives on the adoption experience, as well as further information on specific adoption topics and issues introduced in this book. They include recommendations from adoptive parents, adult adoptees, and adoption professionals.

Resources for General Adoption Information and Support

www.adoptivefamilies.com (web site). Full of information on most aspects of adoption. Publishes the award-winning magazine *Adoptive Families*.

The Evan B. Donaldson Adoption Institute (www.adoptioninstitute. org). A leader in adoption research, education and advocacy.

Adoption Nation by Adam Pertman (New York: Basic Books, 2000). An examination of historical adoption practices and the "revolution" that has occurred in contemporary adoption. Frequently recommended by both adoption professionals and adoptive families.

Local adoption agencies. Many offer classes on specific adoption issues (e.g., transracial adoption, open adoption, etc.) for both adopting families and their extended families. They can also provide support and resources for counseling and education for all members of the adoption circle.

Adoption Mosaic at *www.adoptionmosaic.org.* This Portland, Oregon-based organization offers intelligent, compassionate conversation and education about adoption—for all members of the adoption constellation—via its web site, blog and nationwide trainings.

www.adoptionsupport.org (web site). The Center for Adoption Support and Education (C.A.S.E.) is a non-profit organization dedicated to providing support and education to everyone in the adoption community. In addition to the web site, C.A.S.E. offers workshops, publications, an e-newsletter, seminars and webinars for adoption and general audiences nationwide.

www.chsfs.org (web site). Children's Home Society and Family Services is a nationally-recognized leader in adoption and adoption education. It offers extensive resources and learning opportunities on a broad range of adoption topics for families, their loved ones, and their communities. A helpline (reached via an 800-number or email) offers support and information for post-adoption questions (see web site).

www.growninmyheart.com (web site). The Grown in My Heart (GIMH) site is "a place where all adoptive parents, adoptees, and first moms know they feel safe to air their opinions, regardless of differences." GIMH compiles a semi-annual list of the "Best Adoption, Loss and Infertility Blogs." Categories include: *Informational and Adoptee Rights, Domestic Adoption, International Adoption (subcategories: Asia, South America, Africa and the Caribbean, Europe), First Parents, Adoptees, Infertility, Adoption After Infertility, Foster Care/Foster Care Adoption, Loss,* and *Surrogacy.*

www.tapestrybooks.com; www.perspectivespress.com, www.yeongandyeong.com and *www.emkpress.com* (web sites). Comprehensive resources for books and other media on general and specific topics in adoption.

Adoptee perspectives

Twenty Things Adopted Kids Wish Their Adoptive Parents Knew by Sherrie Eldridge (New York: Dell Publishing, 1999). This book guides my parenting, providing insight into some of my children's potential experiences before they are able to do so themselves.

In Their Own Voices: Transracial Adoptees Tell Their Own Stories by Rita J. Simon and Rhonda M. Roorda (New York: Columbia University Press, 2000). Interviews with African-American and biracial children adopted into Caucasian families.

Lost and Found: A Memoir of Mothers by Kate St. Vincent Vogl (St. Cloud: North Star Press, 2009). An adult adoptee recounts the experience of beginning a relationship with her birthmother following the death of her adoptive mother and the birth of her first child.

Being Adopted: The Lifelong Search for Self by David Brodzinsky (New York: Anchor Books, 1993). A classic adoption text, still recommended by social workers.

www.growninmyheart.com (web site). See list of blogs categorized under *Adoptee Rights* and *Adoptees.*

The Language of Blood by Jane Jeong Trenka (Minneapolis: Graywolf Press, 2005). Memoir of a Korean adoptee raised in the United States, it offers profound insights into international and transracial adoption from the perspective of the adoptee.

Adoption Mosaic at *www.adoptionmosaic.org.* Also a recommended resource for general adoption information, Adoption Mosaic is an especially strong resource for information and insights into the adoptee perspective.

Birth and foster parents

The Girls Who Went Away by Ann Fessler (New York: Penguin Press, 2006). This book is the result of interviews with dozens of women who were sent to "homes for unwed mothers" or otherwise sent away to give birth and surrender their babies for adoption in America in the 1950s, 60s and 70s. A critically important perspective on adoption.

There Is No Me Without You: One Woman's Odyssey to Rescue Her Country's Children by Melissa Faye Green (New York: Bloomsbury, 2006). Green, an adoptive mother and journalist, writes about Ethiopia, the AIDS crisis and Haregewoin Teferra, who fostered hundreds of Ethiopian children orphaned by AIDS. A powerful book.

I Wish for You a Beautiful Life: Letters from the Korean Birth Mothers of Ae Ran Won to Their Children edited by Sara Dorow (St. Paul: Yeong and Yeong Book Company, 1999).

Another Place at the Table by Kathy Harrison (New York: Jeremy P. Tarcher/Putnam: 2003). This eye-opening memoir offers a personal and honest example of one family's experience of providing foster care to children, some of whom they adopted.

www.growninmyheart.com (web site). See blog category *First Parents*.

Transracial and cross-cultural adoption

In Their Parents' Voices: Reflections on Raising Transracial Adoptees by Rita J. Simon and Rhonda M. Roorda (New York: Columbia University Press, 2007). Follow-up to *In Their Own Voices: Transracial Adoptees Tell Their Own Stories* (above).

Cross-Cultural Adoption: How to Answer Questions from Family, Friends and Community by Amy Coughlin and Caryn Abramowitz (Washington, D.C.: Lifeline Press, 2004). The book's suggestions for answering adoption questions asked by non-adoptive children are great.

"Love Isn't Enough: On Raising a Family in a Colorstruck World," blog at *loveisntenough.com*.

Adoption Mosaic at *www.adoptionmosaic.org*. Education and discussion around transracial and cross-cultural adoption are particular areas of focus for Adoption Mosaic.

Inside Transracial Adoption by Gail Steinberg and Beth Hall (Indianapolis: Perspectives Press, 2000).

Foster care and older child adoption

Adopting the Older Child by Claudia Jewett (Boston: Harvard Common Press, 1979). Another classic adoption text, still relevant to today's adoptive families.

Our Own: Adopting and Parenting the Older Child by Trish Maskew (Morton Grove, IL: Snowcap Press, 2003). A frank discussion of the joys and challenges that may characterize older child adoption.

Parenting the Hurt Child: Helping Adoptive Families Heal and Grow by Gregory Keck and Regina Kupecky (Colorado Springs: NavPress, 2009).

Parenting Adopted Adolescents: Understanding and Appreciating Their Journeys by Gregory Keck (Colorado Springs: NavPress, 2009).

www.growninmyheart.com (web site). See blog category *Foster Care/ Foster Care Adoption.*

International adoption

www.adoption.state.gov (web site). The Department of State's web site on intercountry adoption. Includes overviews of international adoption processes by country and information about the Hague Adoption Convention.

www.jcics.org (web site). The mission of the Joint Council on International Children's Services is to advocate on behalf of children in need of permanent families and to promote ethical practices in intercountry adoption. For waiting families and their loved ones, one of the greatest assets of the website is the information provided on adoption issues in sending countries, including up-to-date information on the status of adoption (holds, legal changes, etc.) by country.

"Are Those Kids Yours": American Families With Children Adopted From Other Countries by Cheri Register (New York: Free Press, 1991). Written by the mother of two Korean-born adoptees, the first chapters of this fine book offer an eye-opening and thought-provoking history of adoption practices in the United States and explore the social, ethical, and political implications of

international adoption, both for the adoption community and for society at large.

Beyond Good Intentions: A Mother Reflects on Raising Internationally Adopted Children by Cheri Register (St. Paul: Yeong & Yeong Company, 2005). Register asks adoptive parents to recognize the particular responsibilities required of parents in transracial and international adoptions.

Two Little Girls: A Memoir of Adoption by Theresa Reid (New York: Berkley Trade: 2007). Absorbing and honest recounting of one family's Russian adoptions.

Other topics in adoption

Adopting on Your Own: The Complete Guide to Adopting as a Single Parent by Lee Varon (New York: Farrar, Straus and Giroux, 2000).

www.familyequality.org (web site). The web site of the Family Equality Council is a resource for information and support for LGBT families and their loved ones.

The Open Adoption Book: A Guide to Adoption without Tears by Bruce M. Rappaport (New York: MacMillan, 1992).

"Why Grandma Can't Pick Up the Baby (just yet)" (article) by S.M. Macrae and Karleen Gribble at www.emkpress.com.

"More Than The Blues" (article) by Doris A Landry. Overview of post-adoption depression. Available at www.adoptivefamilies.com/pad (January/February 2010).

www.glossary.adoption.com (web site). Provides a comprehensive list of adoption terminology and definitions.

The Center for Grief, Loss and Transition at www.griefloss.org. Visit the web site for lists of resources and readings on grief and loss.

Adoption in the Movies. Reviews of 27 adoption-themed movies, including discussion questions and points to consider. A great tool for sparking conversations. Available at www.adoptionmosaic.org.

Books about adoption, diversity, and family for children

The Colors of Us by Karen Katz (New York: Henry Holt and Company, 2007).

The Family Book by Todd Parr (New York: Little, Brown Books For Young Readers, 2003).

Whoever You Are by Mem Fox (Orlando: Voyager Books, 2001).

Rosie's Family: An Adoption Story by Lori Rosove (Published in Canada; 2001).

"Helping Classmates Understand Adoption" (article) at www.adoptivefamilies.com

General parenting and child development

The *Touchpoints* series of books on child development by T. Berry Brazelton (Cambridge: Da Capo Press, various editions).

What to Expect the First Year and *What to Expect the Toddler Years* by Heidi Murkoff, Arlene Eisenberg, and Sandee Hathaway (New York: Workman Publishing, 2009 editions).

The Happiest Toddler on the Block by Dr. Harvey Karp (New York: Bantam, 2008)

Acknowledgments

This book was greatly enhanced by the thoughtful contributions of adoptive parents, their friends and relatives, adult adoptees and adoption professionals. One mother described the adoption community this way: "It's not a cross-section of society. It's a pretty uniformly wonderful group of people." I couldn't say it better myself. Thanks in particular to the lovely group of waiting parents and their loved ones who read and responded to the manuscript for *In on it* just before publication. I hope "waiting" is no longer a part of your equation and that you are now simply "parents," "grandparents," "friends," "aunts" and "uncles."

To all of my smart early readers: Thank you for withstanding my initial (sometimes therapeutic) versions of the book and for doing me the honor of holding me to a high standard. *Each of you* provided comments and suggestions that made this book better.

My thanks to the talented publishing, editing and design professionals who helped this English major go from 8½ x 11 to 5¾ x 8: in particular, Pat Morris, Dorie McClelland, Amy Kirkpatrick, Nell Ytsma, and Kate Hopper. Thank you to Kate Raver, John and Rose Sherman, and Laura Billings Coleman for helping *In on it* reach its readers. And I would be remiss if I did not acknowledge my long indebtedness to our system of public libraries. From writing a junior high report on the French Revolution, to selecting a college, to contemplating adoption:

my search for answers to life's questions often begins with a visit to the library.

Thank you to Bill, whose willingness to be outnumbered by his children in Target, at playgrounds, and on camping trips allowed for some distraction-free writing and thinking time.

Thank you to my own circle of friends, family, teachers, colleagues and caregivers, for allowing me to use our example and for your continued support along an ongoing journey.

Thank you to three brave women. Thank you to the people who work on behalf of children and their families around the world.

Index

About the author

Elisabeth O'Toole is a writer and mother of three children through adoption. She holds degrees from Northwestern University and Colorado State University and her professional experience includes roles in business, education, and with non-profit organizations. She resides with her family at various points on the continuum of calm and chaos in St. Paul, Minnesota.